Finish Line for ELLs

English Proficiency Practice

Credits

Illustrations by Doris Ettlinger and Laurie Conley

Photos: Cover and title page: *city girls, boy with skateboard,* BananaStock/Punchstock; *boy reading, girls listening,* Image Source/Punchstock; Page 123: www.istockphoto.com/Curt_Pickens; Page 124: www.photos.com; Page 125: www.shutterstock.com, Rebecca Abell; Page 127: *library,* Library of Congress, David Sharpe; *floorplan,* Thomas Jefferson Foundation, Monticello; Page 128: *map,* en.wikipedia.org; Page 129: *plow, book stand,* Thomas Jefferson Foundation, Monticello; Page 130: en.wikipedia.org; Page 136: www.istockphoto.com/AlexFox; Page 137: www.istockphoto.com/Kovalus; Page 138: www.istockphoto.com/video1

Continental Press, Inc. and the *Finish Line for ELLs* materials are neither affiliated with nor endorsed by any collaborative state organization.

ISBN 978-0-8454-5837-2

Copyright © 2010 The Continental Press, Inc.

No part of this publication may be reproduced in any form or by any means, electronic, mechanical, photocopying, recording, or otherwise, without the prior written permission of the publisher. All rights reserved. Printed in the United States of America.

Table of Contents

About *Finish Line for ELLs: English Proficiency Practice, Grade 4* 7

Unit 1 LISTENING 9

    Model Lesson Academic Science: At the Pet Store 10

        Lesson 1 Conversational Language. 13
          Folder A Personal Information

        Lesson 2 Academic Language Arts 17
          Folder B Main Idea and Details

        Lesson 3 Academic Mathematics 21
          Folder C Equivalent Fractions

        Lesson 4 Academic Social Studies 24
          Folder D Historical Leaders

        Lesson 5 Academic Science. 28
          Folder E States of Matter

        Lesson 6 Conversational Language. 32
          Folder A Leisure Activities

        Lesson 7 Academic Language Arts 36
          Folder B Fable—Story Elements

        Lesson 8 Academic Mathematics 40
          Folder C Money

        Lesson 9 Academic Social Studies 45
          Folder D National Symbols

        Lesson 10 Academic Science. 48
          Folder E Living Systems

Unit 2 READING 53

Model Lesson Academic Science: Caring for Pets 54

Lesson 11 Conversational Language 57
Folder A Informational Text—Opinions

Lesson 12 Academic Mathematics 61
Folder B Place Value

Lesson 13 Academic Science 65
Folder C Energy—Batteries

Lesson 14 Academic Language Arts 68
Folder D Realistic Fiction—Sequence

Lesson 15 Academic Social Studies 71
Folder E America's Story

Lesson 16 Conversational Language 74
Folder A Rules and Procedures

Lesson 17 Academic Mathematics 78
Folder B Time

Lesson 18 Academic Science 82
Folder C Energy—Heat

Lesson 19 Academic Language Arts 85
Folder D Fluency/Self-Monitoring Strategies

Lesson 20 Academic Social Studies 89
Folder E Time Zones

Unit 3 WRITING..**93**

    Model Lesson Academic Science: The Needs of Living Things.............**94**

        Lesson 21 Conversational Language...........................**96**
          Folder A Rules and Procedures

        Lesson 22 Academic Mathematics.............................**98**
          Folder B Area

        Lesson 23 Academic Science...............................**101**
          Folder C States of Matter

        Lesson 24 Conversational Language and
                    Academic Language Arts...........................**103**
          Folder D Leisure Activities

        Lesson 25 Conversational Language..........................**109**
          Folder A Directions

        Lesson 26 Academic Mathematics............................**111**
          Folder B Percent

        Lesson 27 Academic Science...............................**114**
          Folder C Body Systems

        Lesson 28 Academic Language Arts and Social Studies............**116**
          Folder D Basic Economics

Unit 4 SPEAKING..121

    Model Lesson Academic Science: Animals in Our Neighborhood.........**122**

        Lesson 29 Conversational Language............................**123**
        Folder A Personal Experiences

        Lesson 30 Academic Language Arts and Social Studies............**126**
        Folder B Historical Figures

        Lesson 31 Academic Mathematics and Science...................**131**
        Folder C Food and Nutrition

        Lesson 32 Conversational Language............................**136**
        Folder A Health and Safety

        Lesson 33 Academic Language Arts and Social Studies............**139**
        Folder B Communities and Regions

        Lesson 34 Academic Mathematics and Science...................**144**
        Folder C Weather Patterns

About *Finish Line for ELLs: English Proficiency Practice*

The *Finish Line for ELLs: English Proficiency Practice* workbook was developed to help teachers prepare English language learners in grade 4 for similar items found on English language proficiency assessments, such as ACCESS for ELLs® test developed by the WIDA® Consortium, ELDA, NYSESLAT, and individual state tests based on the TESOL standards. By using this workbook, students will become familiar with the types of questions they will face on testing day: multiple choice, written response, and oral response. The book is divided into four units, each one addressing a language domain: speaking, listening, reading, and writing. The content in the listening, reading, and writing units is written for students with developing proficiency levels, overlapping the intermediate, intermediate high, and advanced levels. The lessons in the speaking unit use adaptive questioning to move through five proficiency levels: beginner, intermediate, intermediate high, advanced, and advanced high.

Each unit begins with a model problem to work through with the students. The lessons in each unit are organized by theme folder, each one addressing a specific context for language acquisition: conversational language, academic language arts, academic mathematics, academic science, and academic social studies.

Unit	Basic Format	Question Type	Scoring
Listening	Students listen to information read by the teacher or on an audio CD and then answer questions.	Multiple choice	• Fill in responses in book or use answer sheets
Reading	Students read sentences or passages and respond to questions.	Multiple choice	• Fill in responses in book or use answer sheets
Writing	Students read text and use graphics to formulate ideas in order to write answers to constructed response questions.	Written response	• Write answers to questions in book • Rubrics provided in back of teacher's edition
Speaking	Students use graphic clues to help them speak in response to questions asked by the teacher.	Oral response	• Scored by teacher during administration • Rubrics provided in back of teacher's edition

An accompanying annotated teacher's edition provides answer keys, directions for administering each lesson, and comprehensive skill activities to provide even more practice. Additional teacher support materials in the Appendix include: parent letters in multiple languages, answer sheets with rubrics, and a chart that connects the skills addressed in each unit to workbooks developed by Continental Press that may be used to extend practice to promote English language proficiency.

WIDA and ACCESS for ELLs are registered trademarks of the Board of Regents of the University of Wisconsin System.

 # UNIT 1 LISTENING

Each lesson in this unit focuses on a specific content topic:

1. Conversational language
2. The language of Academic Language Arts
3. The language of Academic Mathematics
4. The language of Academic Science
5. The language of Academic Social Studies

In this unit, you will:

- read and listen to a short story about a picture told in familiar language
- listen to a question
- make out key words in the question
- keep the question in your mind
- listen to and read answer choices
- use picture clues to answer a question
- mark the correct answer

Listen carefully and try to do the best you can!

Model Lesson

ACADEMIC SCIENCE:
At the Pet Store

At the Pet Store

UNIT 1 Listening

Model Lesson

ACADEMIC SCIENCE: At the Pet Store

1.

MODEL LESSON — UNIT 1 Listening — 11

Model Lesson

ACADEMIC SCIENCE:
At the Pet Store

2. Ⓐ A kitten

   Ⓑ A rabbit

   Ⓒ A puppy

   Ⓓ A bird

LISTENING: Conversational Language

Personal Information

All About Alma

LESSON 1 — UNIT 1 Listening

FOLDER A

LISTENING: Conversational Language

Personal Information

1.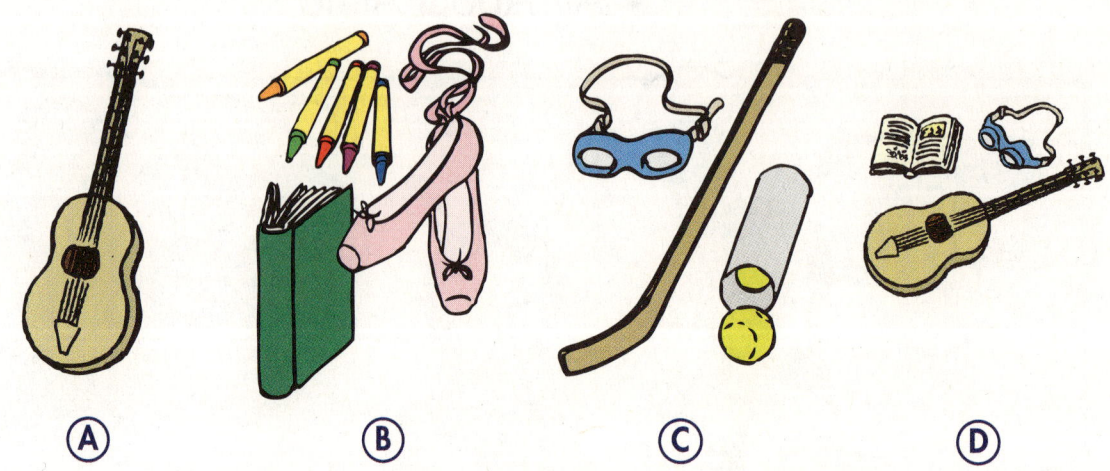

2.

14 UNIT 1 Listening LESSON 1

© The Continental Press, Inc. **DUPLICATING THIS MATERIAL IS ILLEGAL.**

LISTENING: Conversational Language

Folder A

Personal Information

3.

Ⓐ Alma gives the name of her favorite book.

Ⓑ Alma gives information about her dog.

Ⓒ Alma gives information about her birthday.

Ⓓ Alma gives the name of her best friend.

FOLDER A

LISTENING: Conversational Language

Personal Information

4.

Ⓐ "My house has three bedrooms and a big backyard. I call my cousins on the phone."

Ⓑ "My cell phone is purple. My house is blue and white."

Ⓒ "I live at 814 Daffodil Drive. You can call me at 717-555-1212."

Ⓓ "My friend Jessie lives in San Jose. I call her every Saturday."

FOLDER B

LISTENING: Academic Language Arts

Main Idea and Details

The Dinner Party

LESSON 2   UNIT 1 Listening   17

FOLDER B

LISTENING: Academic Language Arts

Main Idea and Details

1.
   Ⓐ   Ⓑ   Ⓒ   Ⓓ

2.
   Ⓐ   Ⓑ   Ⓒ   Ⓓ

18 UNIT 1 Listening   LESSON 2
© The Continental Press, Inc. **DUPLICATING THIS MATERIAL IS ILLEGAL.**

LISTENING: Academic Language Arts

Main Idea and Details

3.
   (A) Folami brought homemade rye bread.

   (B) Gina brought peach pie for dessert.

   (C) Lionel brought a spinach and tomato salad.

   (D) Anne wore a new purple blouse.

LISTENING: Academic Language Arts

Main Idea and Details

4. 	Ⓐ The friends had a good time together.

　　Ⓑ During dinner, they talked about books they had read.

　　Ⓒ They laughed at each other's jokes.

　　Ⓓ After dinner, they played charades.

FOLDER C — LISTENING: Academic Mathematics

Equivalent Fractions

Serving Pizza

LISTENING: Academic Mathematics

Equivalent Fractions

1.

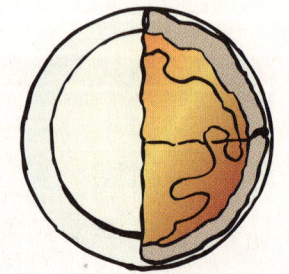 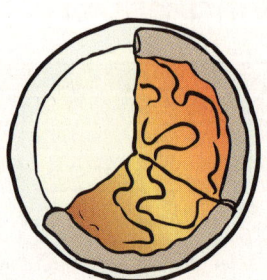 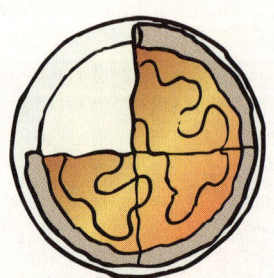 

$\frac{1}{2}$ $\frac{2}{3}$ $\frac{3}{4}$ $\frac{2}{8}$

Ⓐ   Ⓑ   Ⓒ   Ⓓ

2.

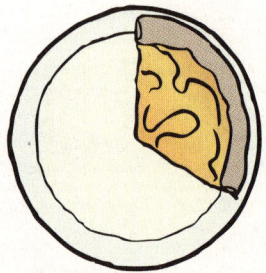 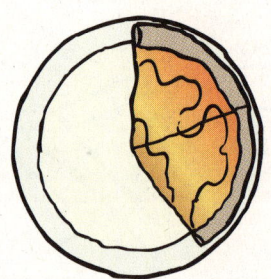 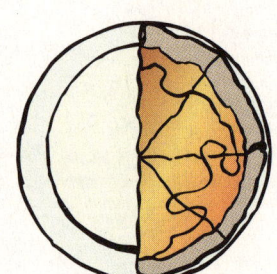 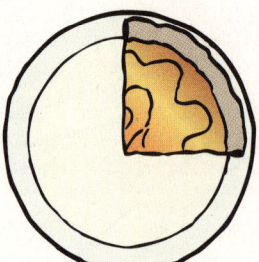

$\frac{1}{3}$ $\frac{2}{5}$ $\frac{4}{8}$ $\frac{1}{4}$

Ⓐ   Ⓑ   Ⓒ   Ⓓ

LISTENING: Academic Mathematics

Equivalent Fractions

3. Ⓐ Shares
   Ⓑ Plates
   Ⓒ Pepperoni
   Ⓓ Friends

4. Ⓐ $\frac{5}{8}$
   Ⓑ $\frac{3}{4}$
   Ⓒ $\frac{4}{4}$
   Ⓓ $\frac{8}{6}$

LESSON 3 — UNIT 1 Listening — 23

FOLDER D
Historical Leaders

LISTENING: Academic Social Studies

Daniel Boone and the Frontier

FOLDER D

LISTENING: Academic Social Studies

Historical Leaders

1.

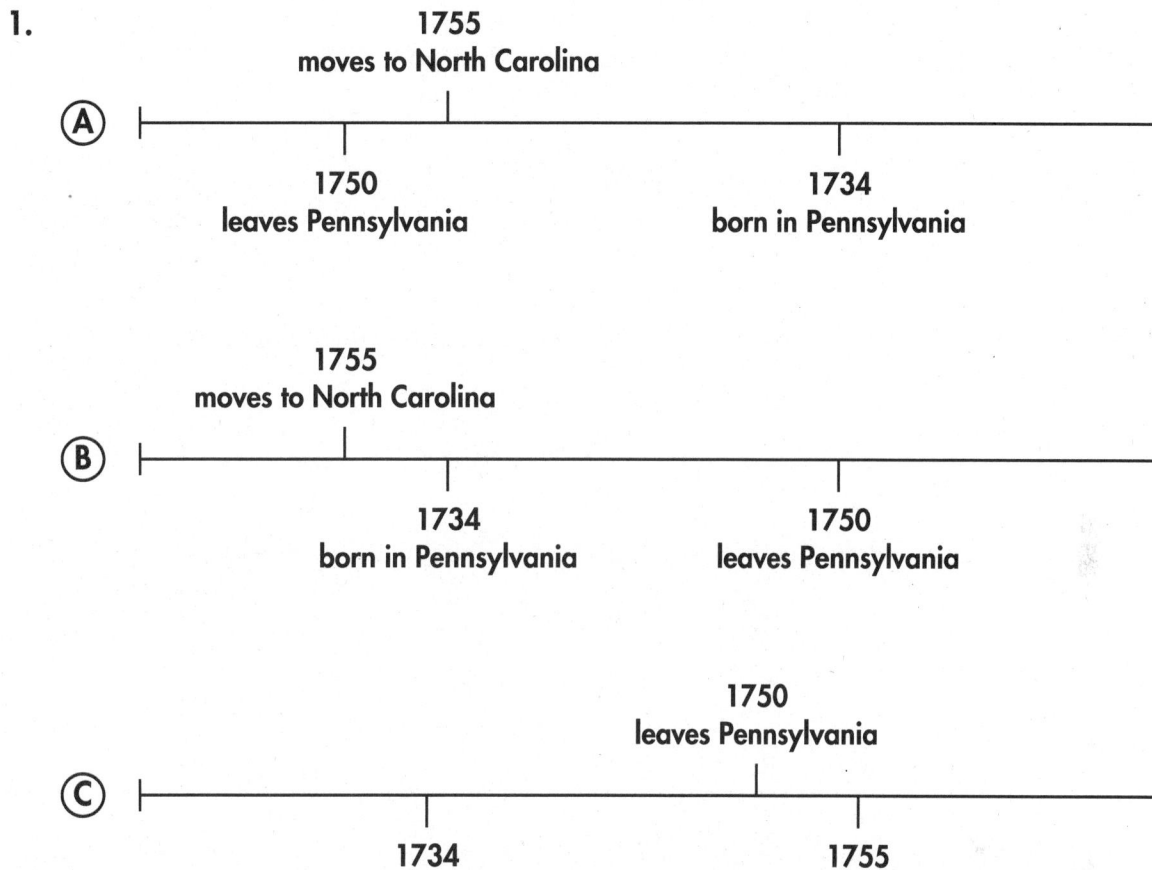

Ⓐ
- 1755 moves to North Carolina
- 1750 leaves Pennsylvania
- 1734 born in Pennsylvania

Ⓑ
- 1755 moves to North Carolina
- 1734 born in Pennsylvania
- 1750 leaves Pennsylvania

Ⓒ
- 1750 leaves Pennsylvania
- 1734 born in Pennsylvania
- 1755 moves to North Carolina

LESSON 4 UNIT 1 Listening 25

FOLDER **D**

LISTENING: Academic Social Studies

Historical Leaders

2.

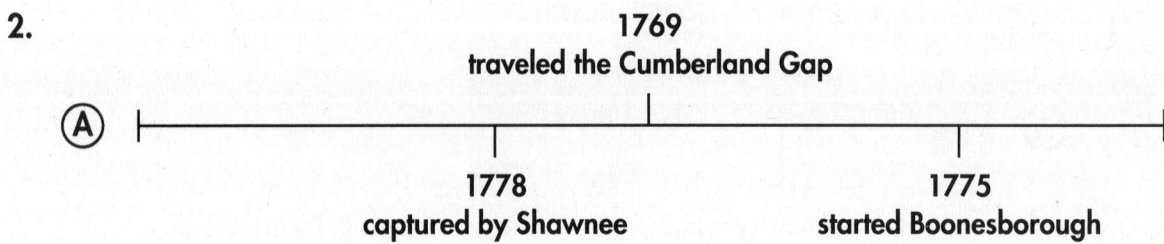

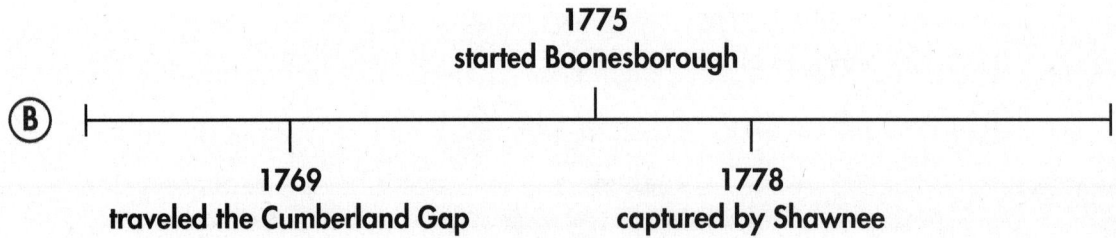

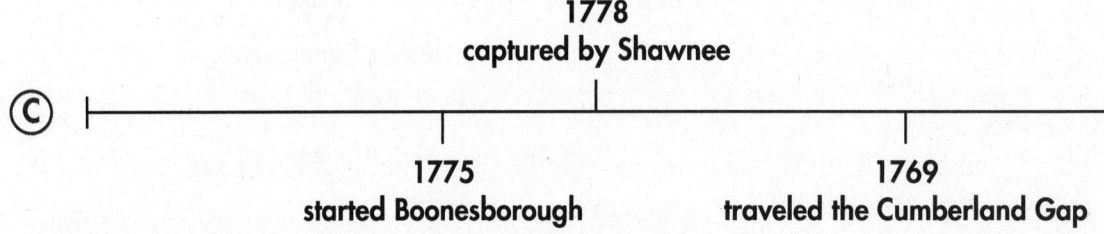

26 | **UNIT 1 Listening** | **LESSON 4**

© The Continental Press, Inc. **DUPLICATING THIS MATERIAL IS ILLEGAL.**

FOLDER D

LISTENING: Academic Social Studies

Historical Leaders

3. (A) He impressed the chief.

   (B) He traveled 160 miles.

   (C) He warned everyone.

   (D) He was captured.

4. (A) People followed him because he was an adventurer.

   (B) People followed him because he was a poor hunter.

   (C) People followed him because he got lost all of the time.

   (D) People followed him because he invited them to come along.

LESSON 4 UNIT 1 Listening 27

FOLDER E

States of Matter

LISTENING: Academic Science

FOLDER E

States of Matter

LISTENING: Academic Science

1.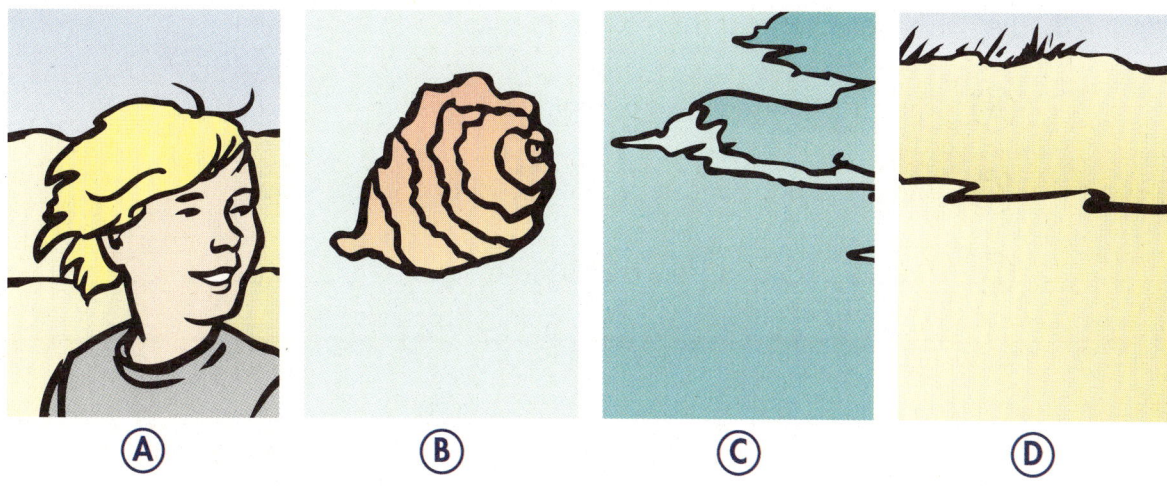

2.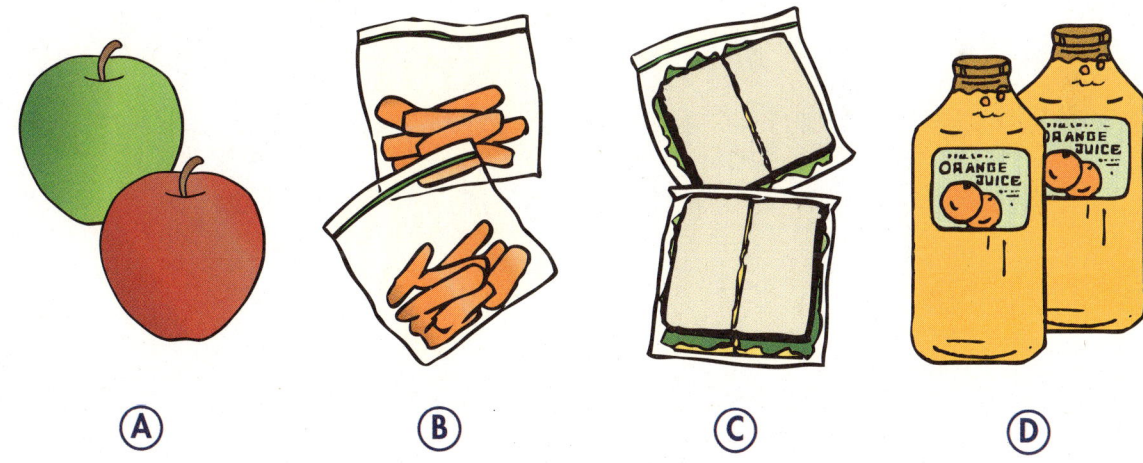

LESSON 5   UNIT 1 Listening

FOLDER E — LISTENING: Academic Science

States of Matter

3. Ⓐ The ice changed from a gas to a solid.

   Ⓑ The ice changed from a liquid to a gas.

   Ⓒ The ice changed from a small solid to a large solid.

   Ⓓ The ice changed from a solid to a liquid.

FOLDER E		LISTENING: Academic Science
	States of Matter	

4.

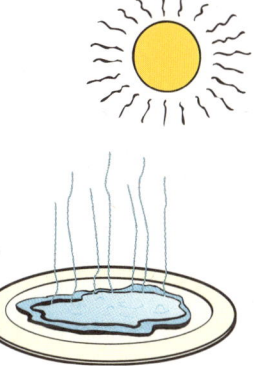

Ⓐ The water changed into a gas and went up into the air.

Ⓑ The water changed back into solid ice.

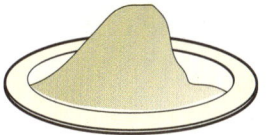

Ⓒ The water changed into a different liquid.

Ⓓ The water changed to snow.

LESSON 5   UNIT 1 Listening

LISTENING: Conversational Language

Leisure Activities

Rainy Day Activities

FOLDER A

LISTENING: Conversational Language

Leisure Activities

1.

  Ⓐ   Ⓑ   Ⓒ

2.

  Ⓐ   Ⓑ   Ⓒ   Ⓓ

◀ LESSON 6   UNIT 1 Listening | 33

© The Continental Press, Inc.   **DUPLICATING THIS MATERIAL IS ILLEGAL.**

LISTENING: Conversational Language

Leisure Activities

3.

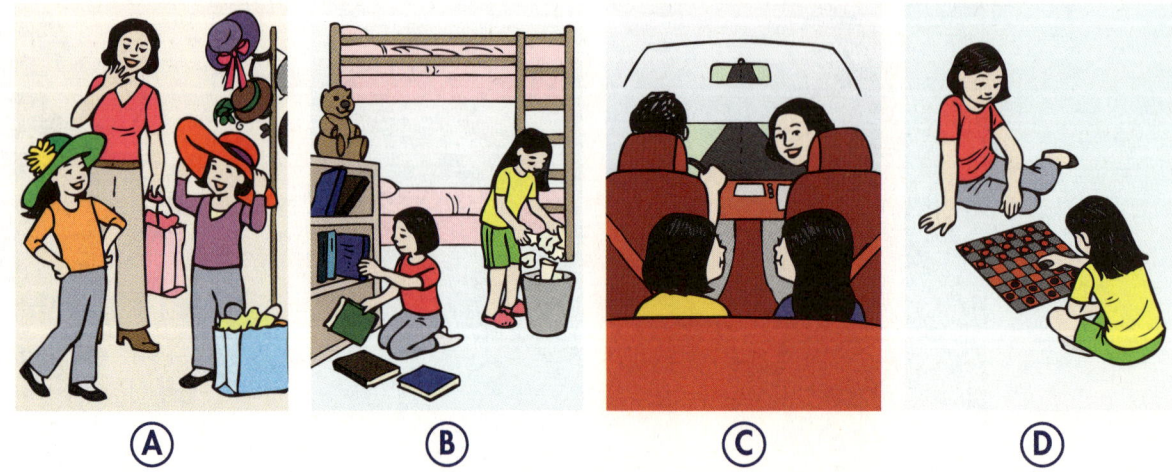

Ⓐ   Ⓑ   Ⓒ   Ⓓ

34 UNIT 1 Listening   LESSON 6

FOLDER A — LISTENING: Conversational Language

Leisure Activities

4.

- **A** The children will bake cookies.
- **B** The children will plant flowers.
- **C** The children will do their homework.
- **D** The children will play soccer.

LESSON 6   UNIT 1 Listening   35

© The Continental Press, Inc.   **DUPLICATING THIS MATERIAL IS ILLEGAL.**

FOLDER B

LISTENING: Academic Language Arts

Fable—Story Elements

The Winner

UNIT 1 Listening — LESSON 7

LISTENING: Academic Language Arts

Fable—Story Elements

1.

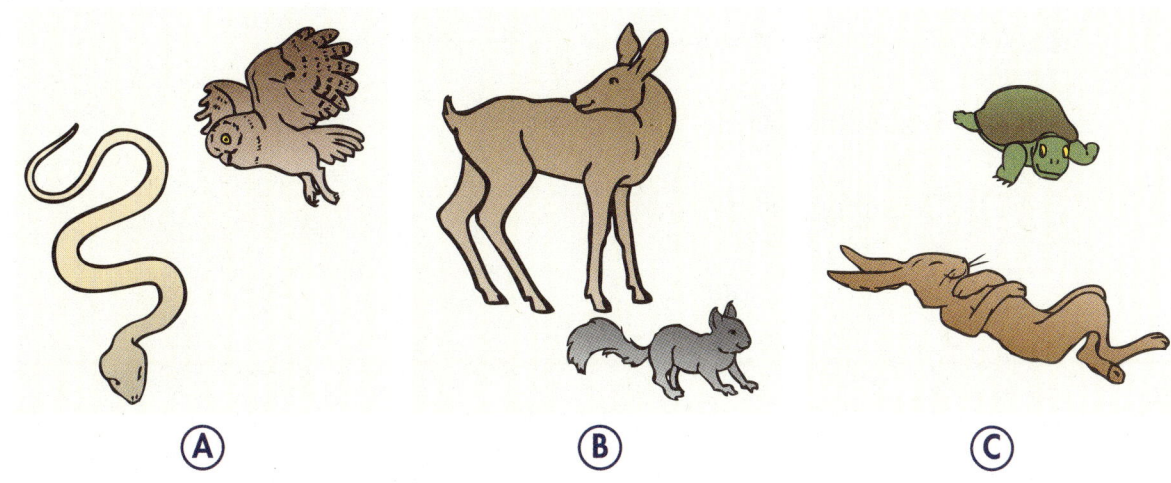

Ⓐ Ⓑ Ⓒ

2.

Ⓐ Ⓑ Ⓒ Ⓓ

LESSON 7   UNIT 1 Listening   37
© The Continental Press, Inc.   DUPLICATING THIS MATERIAL IS ILLEGAL.

Fable—Story Elements

3. Ⓐ They will get to the finish line at the same time.

   Ⓑ The rabbit will win.

   Ⓒ The rabbit will go back to sleep.

   Ⓓ The turtle will win.

 LISTENING: Academic Language Arts

Fable—Story Elements

4.

Event	Lesson
Rabbit and Turtle start the race.	?
Rabbit takes a nap.	?
Turtle moves slowly and keeps going.	?
Turtle wins the race.	?

(A) It's better to go slowly and reach your goal than to start quickly and stop.

(B) You can do your best if you work quickly.

(C) Taking a nap can help you get your work done better and faster.

(D) It's a good idea to stay out of the rain.

LESSON 7 　　　　　　　　　　　UNIT 1 Listening　39

FOLDER C

Money

LISTENING: Academic Mathematics

A Pocket Full of Coins

FOLDER C — Money

LISTENING: Academic Mathematics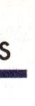

1.
   Ⓐ   Ⓑ   Ⓒ   Ⓓ

LESSON 8   UNIT 1 Listening   41

LISTENING: Academic Mathematics

Money

2.

Ⓐ He picks up two dimes.

Ⓑ He picks up two nickels.

Ⓒ He picks up two quarters.

Ⓓ He picks up two pennies.

LISTENING: Academic Mathematics

Money

3.

(A) He picks up three pennies and one quarter.

(B) He picks up three dimes and one penny.

(C) He picks up three quarters and one penny.

(D) He picks up three nickels and one dime.

LISTENING: Academic Mathematics

Money

4. Ⓐ Tony picks up six nickels and one penny.

   Ⓑ Tony picks up five dimes and one quarter.

   Ⓒ Tony picks up twenty pennies, one nickel, and three dimes.

   Ⓓ Tony picks up one quarter, one dime, and one nickel.

FOLDER D

LISTENING: Academic Social Studies

National Symbols

National Symbols

LESSON 9 — UNIT 1 Listening — 45

FOLDER D

LISTENING: Academic Social Studies

National Symbols

1.

   Ⓐ   Ⓑ   Ⓒ

2.

   Ⓐ   Ⓑ   Ⓒ

46   **UNIT 1** Listening   LESSON 9

© The Continental Press, Inc.   **DUPLICATING THIS MATERIAL IS ILLEGAL.**

FOLDER D

LISTENING: Academic Social Studies

National Symbols

3. Ⓐ A fish
   Ⓑ 6 arrows
   Ⓒ A feather
   Ⓓ An olive branch

4. Ⓐ The U. S. flag
   Ⓑ The Liberty Bell
   Ⓒ A bald eagle
   Ⓓ A rose

LESSON 9   UNIT 1 Listening   47
© The Continental Press, Inc.   **DUPLICATING THIS MATERIAL IS ILLEGAL.**

LISTENING: Academic Science

Living Systems

Plant Parts for Lunch

LISTENING: Academic Science

Living Systems

1.

Ⓐ　　　Ⓑ　　　Ⓒ　　　Ⓓ

LESSON 10 　　　UNIT 1 Listening　　49

FOLDER E

Living Systems

LISTENING: Academic Science

2.

- Ⓐ You can pick the fruit and eat it.
- Ⓑ The seeds grow inside the fruit.
- Ⓒ Flowers bloom on the plant.
- Ⓓ The plant grows to become a tree.

FOLDER E

Living Systems

LISTENING: Academic Science

3.

- **A** Cut up the carrot into pieces.
- **B** Wash it carefully.
- **C** Dig up the carrot.
- **D** Put the carrot pieces in the soup pot.

LISTENING: Academic Science

Living Systems

4. Ⓐ You will eat a cabbage leaf.

   Ⓑ You will eat an ear of corn.

   Ⓒ You will eat a green bean.

   Ⓓ You will eat an apple.

UNIT 2 READING

Each lesson in this unit focuses on a specific content topic:
1. Conversational language
2. The language of Academic Language Arts
3. The language of Academic Mathematics
4. The language of Academic Science
5. The language of Academic Social Studies

In this unit, you will:
- read a chart or short story with several paragraphs
- understand questions about the text
- use picture clues and key words to answer questions about
    - reading graphic organizers
    - identifying whole numbers
    - comparing and contrasting
    - understanding sequence
    - finding main idea and details
    - making predictions
    - understanding vocabulary
- mark the correct answer

Read carefully and try to do the best you can!

Model Lesson

ACADEMIC SCIENCE:
Caring for Pets

Caring for Pets

What We Will Do	Kind of Pet	Times
Play with String	Kittens	11 A.M.–11:30 A.M.
Feed the Animals	Rabbits	12:00 noon–12:30 P.M.
Play with a Ball	Puppies	1:00 P.M.–1:30 P.M.
Give a Bath	Puppies	1:00 P.M.–1:30 P.M.

Model Lesson

ACADEMIC SCIENCE:
Caring for Pets

1. Melissa wants to help feed the rabbits. Look at the chart. What time will she need to be at the store for that event?

    Ⓐ 11 A.M.

    Ⓑ 12 noon

    Ⓒ 1:30 P.M.

2. Look at the schedule of events at the pet store. What sentence tells something true about the show schedule?

   A All of the events happen at the same time.

   B Only the puppies have play time.

   C The puppies play and get baths during the same time.

   D There are no events at the store after 12 noon.

READING: Conversational Language

Informational Text—Opinions

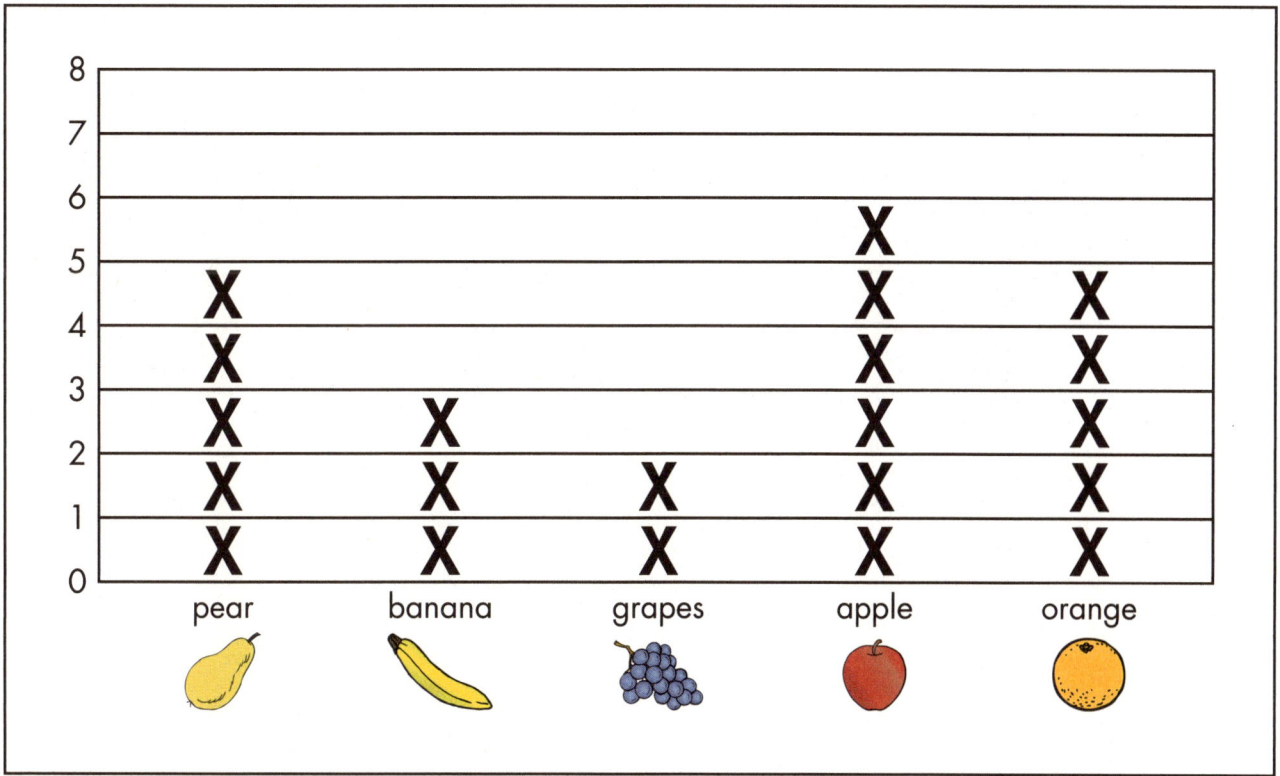

Fruit Favorites

FOLDER A

READING: Conversational Language

Informational Text—Opinions

1. All students have given their opinions about their favorite fruit. Which fruit is the favorite of six students?

58 | UNIT 2 Reading

LESSON 11

© The Continental Press, Inc. **DUPLICATING THIS MATERIAL IS ILLEGAL.**

READING: Conversational Language

Informational Text—Opinions

2. Look carefully at the bar graph that shows favorite fruits. Which sentence below is true about the bar graph?

   Ⓐ Eight students said that bananas are their favorite fruit.

   Ⓑ No one said that apples are their favorite fruit.

   Ⓒ Two students said that grapes are their favorite fruit.

   Ⓓ Three students said that pears are their favorite fruit.

READING: Conversational Language

 Informational Text—Opinions

3. Look at the bar graph of favorite fruits again. Which fruits are the most and least favorite?

  Ⓐ Bananas and apples

  Ⓑ Apples and grapes

  Ⓒ Grapes and pears

  Ⓓ Oranges and apples

FOLDER B — Place Value

READING: Academic Mathematics

Every Place Has Its Value

Sometimes large numbers with many places can seem confusing. In 2000, the population of the United States was two hundred eighty-one million, four hundred twenty-one thousand, nine hundred six people. That's the word for this number. The standard form of the number is 281,421,906.

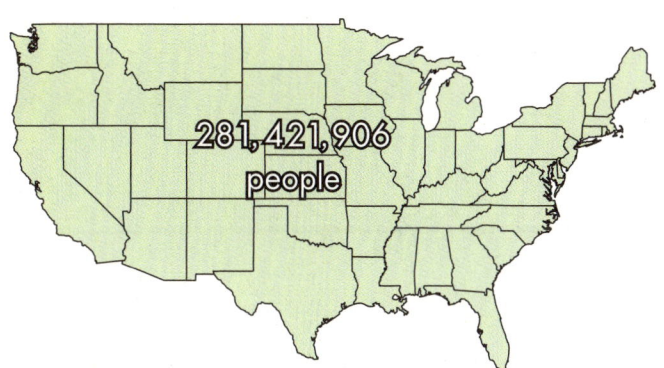

A place value chart can help you read or write large numbers. Each of the digits in a number has a value. The value is based on its position, or place. This is called place value. Look at the place value chart to the right. It shows the number of people in the United States.

Each value of each place is ten times the value of the next place to the right. So a ten is worth ten ones. A hundred is worth 10 tens, and so on.

The places on the chart are grouped by threes into periods. The lowest three places are the ones, tens, and hundreds. They make up the ones period. The next three places are the thousands period. The third period is the millions. Now look at the number in standard form. These periods on the chart are in the same places as the commas in the number. Commas separate the place-value periods in the word form, too.

LESSON 12   UNIT 2 Reading   61

© The Continental Press, Inc.   **DUPLICATING THIS MATERIAL IS ILLEGAL.**

Place Value

READING: Academic Mathematics

1. What is the value of the 4 in the number 281,421,906?

   (A) 400,000

   (B) 4,000

   (C) 400

   (D) 4

2. What is the value of the underlined digit in the number 2̲81,421,906?

   (A) 2

   (B) 20

   (C) 2,000

   (D) 200,000,000

FOLDER B

READING: Academic Mathematics

Place Value

3. Look at the place value chart. Which two number words go in the **Ones Period?**

Millions Period			Thousands Period			Ones Period		
Hundred Millions	Ten Millions	Millions	Hundred Thousands	Ten Thousands	Thousands			Ones
2	8	1	4	2	1	9	0	6

(A) Ten Millions, Thousands

(B) Millions, Ten Thousands

(C) Hundred Millions, Hundred Thousands

(D) Hundreds, Tens

LESSON 12 UNIT 2 Reading 63

READING: Academic Mathematics

FOLDER B — Place Value

4. Which number is larger: *three hundred seventy-six million, two hundred ninety-four thousand, eight hundred fifteen* or *eight hundred fifteen million, two hundred ninety-four thousand, three hundred seventy-six?*

   Which number below is the same as that word name?

   Ⓐ 294,815,736

   Ⓑ 376,294,815

   Ⓒ 736,815,294

   Ⓓ 815,294,376

READING: Academic Science

Energy—Batteries

Batteries

Electricity is a kind of energy. It can be saved in a battery. A battery stores or saves electricity. Then the electricity can be used at a later time. Batteries come in many sizes, weights, and shapes. Some are small, light, and round. A battery can be as small as your fingernail—or even smaller! Others are large, heavy prisms.

Today, gasoline makes most cars go. But some new cars, called hybrids, are different. First, they use gas to move. As the car moves, it makes energy. The energy goes to a special battery. The battery saves the energy. Then the car switches from using gas to using the battery to run. If the car needs to go faster, it switches back to gas again.

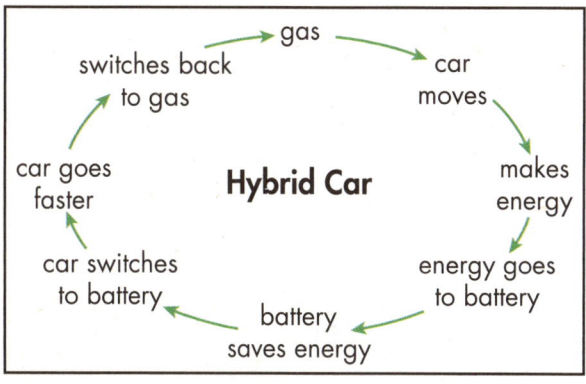

Many machines use batteries to work. A flashlight uses a few small batteries. Cell phones and music players use small batteries, too. A car uses one big battery to make it start. However, animals, people, and plants don't need batteries to live. Look at the chart to see things that do and don't need batteries.

Item	Needs Batteries	Does Not Need Batteries
car	X	
cell phone	X	
person		X
computer	X	
tree		X
flashlight	X	
DVD player	X	

LESSON 13 — UNIT 2 Reading — 65

© The Continental Press, Inc. **DUPLICATING THIS MATERIAL IS ILLEGAL.**

FOLDER C

Energy—Batteries

READING: Academic Science

1. Which picture shows a battery?

  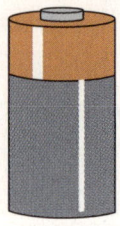

 Ⓐ Ⓑ Ⓒ

READING: Academic Science

Energy—Batteries

2. Look at the diagram of the energy for the car. What happens <u>after</u> the energy goes to the battery?

   Ⓐ The battery saves the energy.

   Ⓑ The car switches back to gas.

   Ⓒ The battery stops working.

   Ⓓ The car has to go faster.

3. Look at the chart on page 65 again. Based on information in the chart, which analogy is true?

   Ⓐ Doesn't need batteries : needs batteries △ computers : cars

   Ⓑ Doesn't need batteries : needs batteries △ living : non-living

   Ⓒ Doesn't need batteries : needs batteries △ person : tree

   Ⓓ Doesn't need batteries : needs batteries △ DVD player : flashlight

Making Cookies With Mom

Mom makes great cookies. I help her make them. It is very easy. First, Mom turns on the oven so it will get hot. Next, we get out all of the ingredients and then we put them on the kitchen table. We use chocolate chips, baking soda, vanilla, butter, eggs, sugar, flour, and salt. I mix butter, vanilla, and sugar in the bowl. Then I break the eggs into the bowl.

Mom measures the rest of the ingredients. She puts in the flour and baking soda, and I mix them in with the sugar mixture. Next, she adds the salt. I stir constantly until the ingredients blend together. Then Mom adds the chocolate chips, and I mix them in. After that, we use a spoon to put the cookie dough on the baking pan. Mom puts the pan in the hot oven.

The cookies bake for about ten minutes. During that time, Mom and I clean up the kitchen. At last, the cookies are done, and Mom takes them out of the oven. We wait about fifteen minutes for them to cool off. Then we put them on a plate. We call the rest of the family in to have cookies and milk. Yum!

READING: Academic Language Arts

Realistic Fiction — Sequence

1. Which event happens <u>first</u> in the story?

Ⓐ

Ⓑ

Ⓒ

2. Which word tells when Mom adds the salt?

Ⓐ Next

Ⓑ Minutes

Ⓒ Dough

Ⓓ Fifteen

LESSON 14 UNIT 2 Reading 69

FOLDER D READING: Academic Language Arts

Realistic Fiction—Sequence

3. What do the boy and his mother do during the time that the cookies bake?

   Ⓐ They get out all of the ingredients.

   Ⓑ They add the chocolate chips to the dough.

   Ⓒ They put the pan in the oven.

   Ⓓ They clean up the kitchen.

4. The person who wrote this story wrote another story. This story is also told using steps in a process. Which topic do you think the story will be about?

   Ⓐ A list of favorite songs

   Ⓑ Silly jokes and riddles

   Ⓒ The names of family members

   Ⓓ Building a birdhouse with Dad

The Erie Canal

Before 1776, Americans lived mostly near the East Coast. By 1817, many had moved west. Travel on land was slow. So merchants used waterways whenever they could. In 1817, the people of New York began building the Erie Canal. A canal is a waterway that connects two bodies of water. The Erie Canal would connect the city of Albany on the Hudson River with the city of Buffalo on Lake Erie.

Workers had to dig the canal by hand. They often worked 14-hour days. The work was very hard. In 1825, the Erie Canal was finished. It was 363 miles long, 40 feet wide, and 4 feet deep. Merchants could now send their products for less money. Travel time was shorter, too.

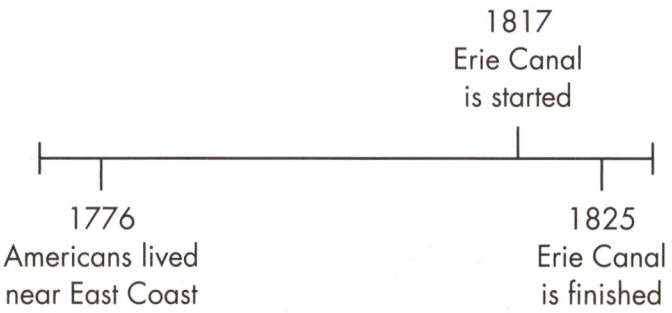

The Erie Canal also helped people get together. The canal's flatboats held up to 100 passengers. People began visiting friends and neighbors who had moved away. For many people, it was their first chance to see other parts of the country.

READING: Academic Social Studies

FOLDER E

America's Story

1. Look at the map again. On which body of water is the city of Albany?

    Ⓐ Albany is on the Hudson River.

    Ⓑ Albany is on Lake Ontario.

    Ⓒ Albany is on the St. Lawrence River.

    Ⓓ Albany is on Lake Erie.

2. Look at the time line again. When was the Erie Canal finished?

    Ⓐ It was finished in 1817.

    Ⓑ It was finished in 1776.

    Ⓒ It was finished in 1825.

    Ⓓ It was finished in 1725.

READING: Academic Social Studies

America's Story

3. What probably happened after the Erie Canal was built?

   (A) People never went anywhere.

   (B) Many more people moved west.

   (C) People wanted to work on the canal.

   (D) Most people did not like the canal.

FOLDER A — Rules and Procedures

READING: Conversational Language

Clay Elementary School Rules

First, Mr. Roy explains what students should do in the cafeteria. "Stay in line at the lunch counter. Slide your tray along the shelf, and put your dishes on it. Pick up your tray after you have all of your food. Hold your tray in two hands as you walk to your table."

Next, Mr. Roy takes the students to the library. He says, "You must be quiet in the library. Ask the librarian for help to reach books on the high shelves. Carefully carry your books to a table or chair. Sit quietly and read or take notes. Make sure you check out any books you want to borrow. Ask for permission if you have to leave the library."

After that, Mr. Roy and the students go to the playground. He tells them, "Playground safety is important. Ask a friend to stand at the bottom of the slide while you go down. If you run, make sure you're not near the swings or in the middle of a ball game. Be sure to share the equipment. Ask for permission if you have to leave the playground."

READING: Conversational Language

Rules and Procedures

1. Mr. Roy explains how the students should behave while they eat lunch. What will they do?

LESSON 16 — UNIT 2 Reading

READING: Conversational Language

Rules and Procedures

2. In the library Fernando found a book and checked it out. Which rule should he follow now?

- Ⓐ Sit quietly and read.
- Ⓑ Ask a librarian for help to reach a high shelf.
- Ⓒ Check out any books you want to borrow.
- Ⓓ Take several books at a time.

READING: Conversational Language

Rules and Procedures

3. Compare the procedures for the library and the playground. Which rule is the same?

   (A) Make sure you're not near the swings when you run.

   (B) Sit quietly and read.

   (C) Ask for permission if you have to leave.

   (D) Share the equipment with other students.

READING: Academic Mathematics

FOLDER B Time

As Time Goes By

Get ready for a vacation! Your plane leaves New York at 3:01 P.M. It arrives in Florida at 6:11 P.M. How long will the flight take? To answer this question, you need to find the elapsed time. That's the difference between the starting and ending times.

Look at the clock on the left. The hands show the starting time, 3:01. Now look at the clock on the right. The hour hand is the short hand. Trace the movement of the hour hand from three o'clock to six o'clock. Three hours have gone by, or elapsed.

Look at the clock on the left. The minute hand is the longer hand. Each small mark between the numbers is equal to one minute. From :01 to :11 is ten minutes.

The elapsed time is 3 hours 10 minutes. That's the total travel time to fly from New York to Florida.

78 | **UNIT 2 Reading** | **LESSON 17**

© The Continental Press, Inc.   **DUPLICATING THIS MATERIAL IS ILLEGAL.**

FOLDER B — Time

READING: Academic Mathematics

1. The plane has landed in Florida. You and your family get your suitcases and rent a car. You drive to your hotel. You get to your hotel at 7:45 P.M. Which clock shows 7:45?

   Ⓐ   Ⓑ   Ⓒ

LESSON 17   UNIT 2 Reading   79

© The Continental Press, Inc.   **DUPLICATING THIS MATERIAL IS ILLEGAL.**

READING: Academic Mathematics

FOLDER B — Time

2. One day you and your family go to the beach. You set up your chairs and umbrellas at 1:00 P.M. You play in the sand, swim, walk, and read books. You leave the beach 4 hours and 30 minutes later. Which clock shows the time you left the beach?

Ⓐ

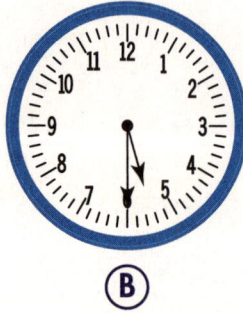
Ⓑ

Ⓒ

READING: Academic Mathematics

FOLDER B

Time

3. The next day, you go with your family to an amusement park. You arrive at 10:00 A.M. You ride on many fast, exciting roller coasters. You have such a good time that you stay at the park until 8:00 P.M. How many hours did you stay at the park?

Ⓐ Elapsed time = 10 hours

Ⓑ Elapsed time = 18 hours

Ⓒ Elapsed time = 2 hours

LESSON 17 | UNIT 2 Reading | 81

READING: Academic Science

Energy—Heat

A "Cool" Way to Make Heat

What do you feel when you stand by a fire? You feel heat. Fire is hot. Fire happens when something burns. A campfire burns wood. Some lamps burn oil. Candles burn wax. Campfires, lamps, and candles all make heat.

You can make heat another way. Rub your hands together fast. Keep doing it. What do you feel? Your hands get warm because you are making heat. You can rub two things together to make heat. This rubbing is called friction.

American Indians made fires. First, they made a hole in a flat piece of wood. They put a stick in the hole. They kept spinning the stick between their hands. The spinning stick would grind off small bits of wood. The friction from the spinning stick made the small bits of wood hot. They made a flame by carefully blowing on the hot bits of wood.

READING: Academic Science

Energy—Heat

1. Which picture shows something that makes heat?

Ⓐ   Ⓑ   Ⓒ

2. Which word in the story means, "rubbing two things together to make heat"?

   Ⓐ Candles

   Ⓑ Spinning

   Ⓒ Friction

   Ⓓ Flame

LESSON 18 UNIT 2 Reading 83

READING: Academic Science

Energy—Heat

3.
| First, they made a hole in a flat piece of wood. |

↓

| They put a stick in the hole. |

↓

| They kept spinning the stick between their hands. |

↓

| The spinning stick would grind off small bits of wood. |

↓

| The friction from the spinning stick made the small bits of wood hot. |

↓

| They made a flame by blowing on the hot bits of wood. |

When making a fire, what did the American Indians do <u>after</u> they made the small wood bits hot?

Ⓐ They put a stick in the hole.

Ⓑ They kept spinning the stick between their hands.

Ⓒ They made a hole in a flat piece of wood.

Ⓓ They made a flame by blowing on the hot bits of wood.

Under the Ocean

Did you ever wonder what it's like deep on the ocean floor?

There are mountains and valleys on the ocean floor. The deepest valley in the ocean is almost seven miles deep. The tallest mountain on Earth is five and a half miles high.

Near the coasts of the continents and islands, the sea is full of life. The water is shallow, or not very deep. What happens in shallow water? The sun warms the water and helps the plants grow. Many fish live there. More than 90 percent of sea life live in the shallow waters near the coastal zone. The resources of the coastal zone are good for people, too. More than 60 percent of the world's people live on or near a seacoast.

Other parts of the ocean are dark and cold. In many places, the water is so deep that no sun can get to the ocean floor. Does anything live on the ocean floor where it is dark and cold? Scientists have discovered that very tiny organisms live there. They are made up of a single cell. They do not eat plants, so they do not need the sun.

READING: Academic Language Arts

Fluency/Self-Monitoring Strategies

1. Read the following sentence from the passage:

   Near the coasts of the continents and islands, the sea is full of life.

   Which picture shows a coast?

Ⓐ

Ⓑ

Ⓒ

READING: Academic Language Arts

Fluency/Self-Monitoring Strategies

2. Read the passage again. What punctuation cue does the author use to show that an answer is in the next sentence?

   Ⓐ The author uses an exclamation point.

   Ⓑ The author uses a question mark.

   Ⓒ The author uses quotation marks.

   Ⓓ The author uses a colon.

3. You may not remember the numbers that tell the percents of sea life and people who live in the coastal zone. Scan paragraph 3 to look for these numbers. Which numbers do you find?

   Ⓐ 100 percent/7 percent

   Ⓑ 10 percent/57 percent

   Ⓒ 30 percent/85 percent

   Ⓓ 90 percent/60 percent

LESSON 19   UNIT 2 Reading   87

© The Continental Press, Inc.   DUPLICATING THIS MATERIAL IS ILLEGAL.

READING: Academic Language Arts

Fluency/Self-Monitoring Strategies

4. You may not remember the information about the size of the deepest valley on the ocean floor. What do you do to find the information?

    Ⓐ Look in the dictionary for a definition of the word "valley."

    Ⓑ Write down the main idea of each of the paragraphs.

    Ⓒ Reread the sentence that compares the valley to a land mountain.

    Ⓓ Find a picture of the fish that live along the coastline.

U.S. Time Zones

The world is divided into 24 time zones. That makes one time zone for each hour of the day. Time in the zones to the east of where you live is later than your time. The time in the zones to the west of where you live is earlier than your time.

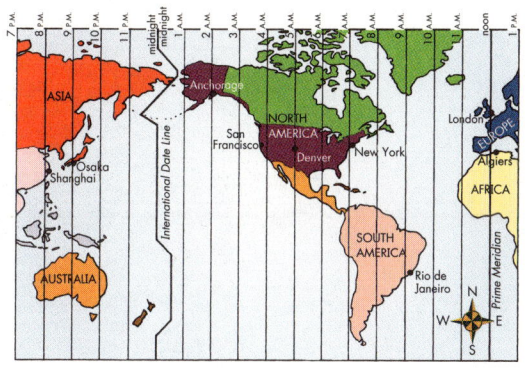

Six of the time zones are in the United States. The U.S. zones are called the Eastern, Central, Mountain, Pacific, Alaska, and Hawaii-Aleutian Time Zones. Another time zone covers the U.S. territories of the U.S. Virgin Islands and Puerto Rico. Look at the map below to see the time zones.

Time Zones of the United States of America

In the last picture, the clock above each time zone tells what time it is there. If it's 8 P.M. in the Eastern Time Zone, it is 7 P.M. in the Central Time Zone, and 6 P.M. in the Mountain Time Zone. In the Pacific Time Zone it's 5 P.M. It's 4 P.M. in the Alaska Time Zone and 3 P.M. in the Hawaii-Aleutian Time Zone.

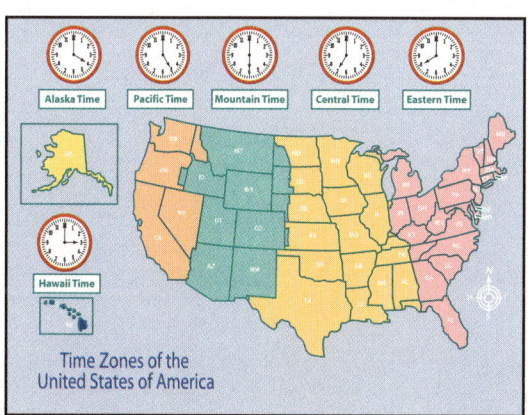

Time Zones of the United States of America

READING: Academic Social Studies

FOLDER E

Time Zones

1. Kate wants to call her grandmother. Kate lives in Pennsylvania (PA). That's in the Eastern Time Zone. Her grandmother lives in Wisconsin. In which time zone is Wisconsin (WI)?

Ⓐ   Ⓑ   Ⓒ

FOLDER E

READING: Academic Social Studies

Time Zones

2. Kate's older sister is working in California (CA). She calls home to her family in Pennsylvania (PA). It's 7:00 A.M. in California. California is west of Pennsylvania. So the time in Pennsylvania will be later. What time is it in Pennsylvania?

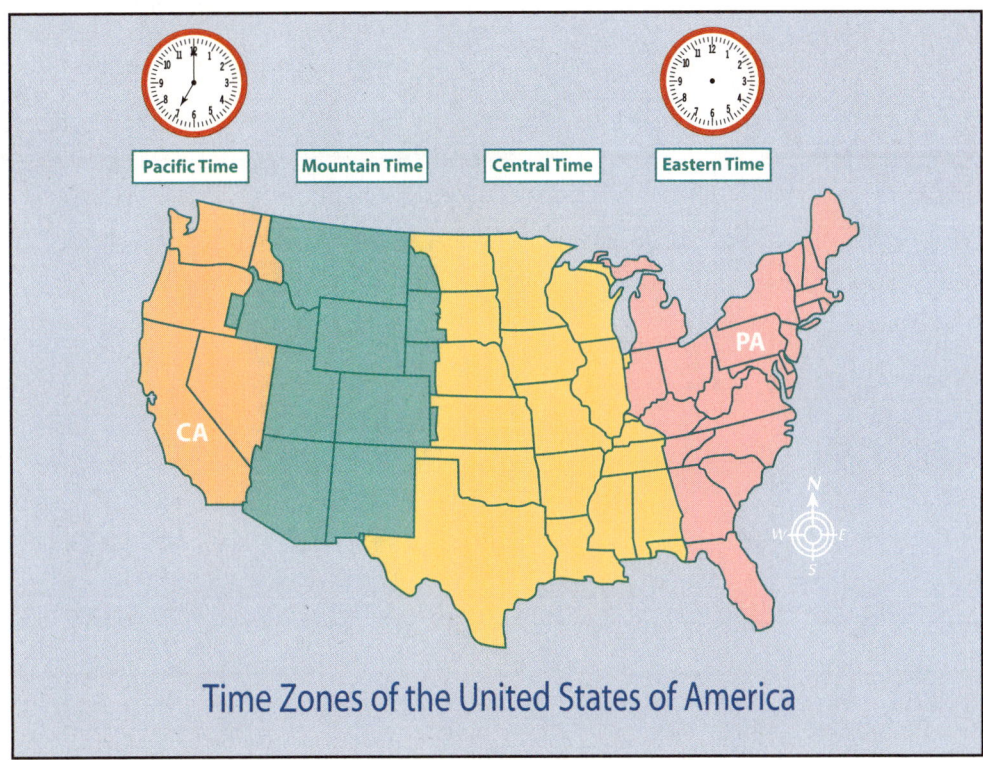

Time Zones of the United States of America

- Ⓐ It is 5:00 A.M. in Pennsylvania.
- Ⓑ It is 9:00 A.M. in Pennsylvania.
- Ⓒ It is 10:00 A.M. in Pennsylvania.
- Ⓓ It is 11:00 A.M. in Pennsylvania.

READING: Academic Social Studies

Time Zones

3. Kate looks at the map of time zones around the world. Which statement about the time zones is true?

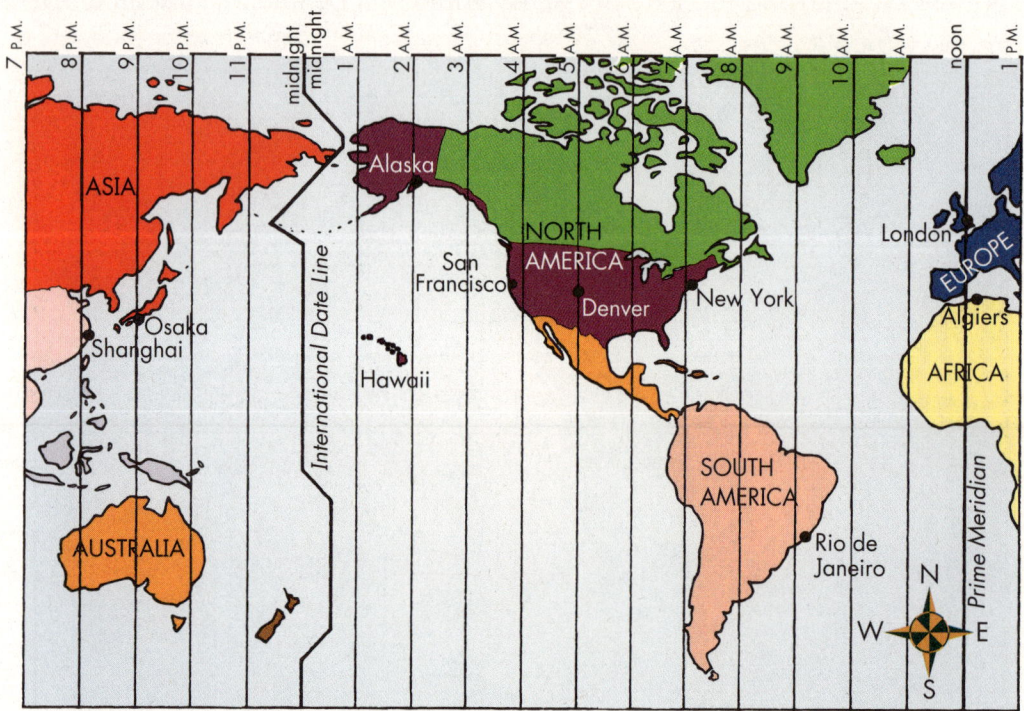

- **A** Africa and Hawaii are in the same time zone.
- **B** Europe and Alaska are only one hour apart.
- **C** There are nine time zones in Australia.
- **D** Parts of North and South America are in the same time zones.

UNIT 3 WRITING

Each lesson in this unit focuses on a specific content topic or topics:

1. Conversational language
2. The language of Academic Language Arts
3. The language of Academic Mathematics
4. The language of Academic Science
5. The language of Academic Social Studies

In this unit, you will:

- read a chart or short story with pictures
- understand questions about the text
- use picture clues and key words to answer questions about the text
- use information in the stories, pictures, and questions to get ideas for writing about a topic
- write ideas as notes
- write about the topic in clear and complete sentences

Write neatly and try to do the best you can!

Model Lesson

ACADEMIC SCIENCE:
The Needs of Living Things

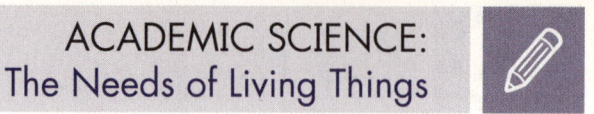

The Needs of Living Things

Animals are living things. Plants are living things. All living things have basic needs in order to survive. Animals need air, water, food, and shelter. Plants need air, water, nutrients, and light. When we take care of animals or plants, we must give them the things they need to help them survive.

Living Things—Animals 	Living Things—Plants 

94 | UNIT 3 Writing | MODEL LESSON

© The Continental Press, Inc.   **DUPLICATING THIS MATERIAL IS ILLEGAL.**

Model Lesson

ACADEMIC SCIENCE:
The Needs of Living Things

Now it's time to write!

What do plants and animals need to survive? Write a paragraph of 5 to 7 sentences about taking care of living things. If you have cared for an animal or plant, write about your experience. Tell what you need to do to help a pet or a plant survive.

___

Check your writing. Ask yourself:

☐ Does my writing make sense?

☐ Did I write in complete sentences?

☐ Did I use correct punctuation and spelling?

☐ Did I write my best?

MODEL LESSON — UNIT 3 Writing — 95

WRITING: **Conversational Language**

Rules and Procedures

Everyone is talking at once.

This student did not do her assignment.

This student is making marks in a classroom library book.

The boy is bothering another student.

96 | **UNIT 3** Writing | **LESSON 21**

© The Continental Press, Inc.   **DUPLICATING THIS MATERIAL IS ILLEGAL.**

WRITING: Conversational Language

Rules and Procedures

Now it's time to write!

What rules do you think would help this fourth-grade class work better? Write 3 to 5 rules for this class. Tell why each rule is important.

___

Check your writing. Ask yourself:

☐ Does my writing make sense?

☐ Did I write in complete sentences?

☐ Did I use correct punctuation and spelling?

☐ Did I write my best?

 FOLDER B

WRITING: Academic Mathematics

Area

The size of a shape's surface is its *area*. There are three steps to find the area of a rectangle. 1) Measure the length of the rectangle. 2) Measure the width of the rectangle. 3) Multiply the length by the width. The total is the area.

Mr. Riley's class will cover their classroom door with paper. They will decorate the paper with drawings about spring. How much paper will they need?

1.

2.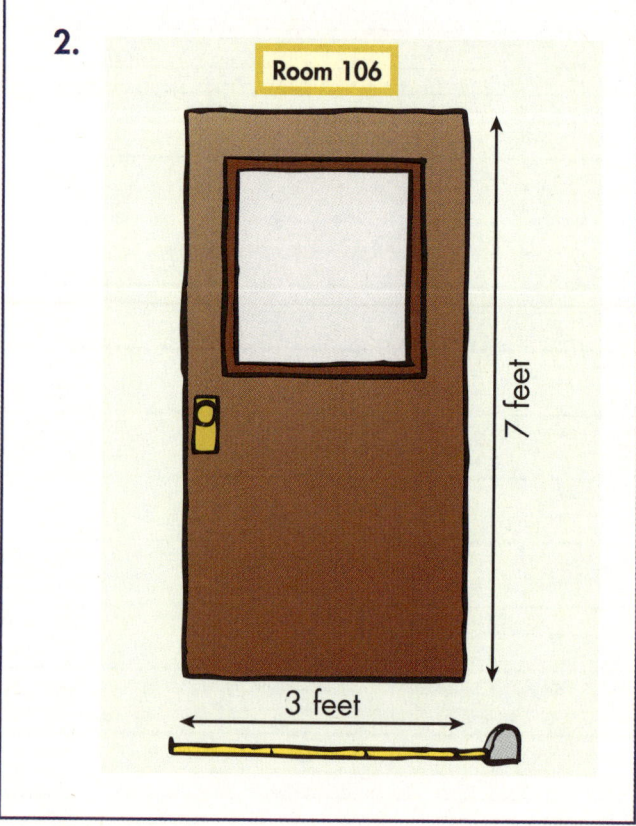

3.
```
     7 feet
    x3 feet
  21 square feet
```

Marisol wrote a paragraph to tell how she solved the problem. She started like this.

First, I measured the length...

98 **UNIT 3** Writing   LESSON 22

© The Continental Press, Inc.   **DUPLICATING THIS MATERIAL IS ILLEGAL.**

WRITING: Academic Mathematics

Area

Now it's time to write!

Mrs. Lee wants to cover the living room floor with carpet. How much carpet will she need? Write 6 to 8 sentences explaining how to solve this problem.

Use the picture below and the model on page 98 to prepare your answer. Write your paragraph on the next page.

1.

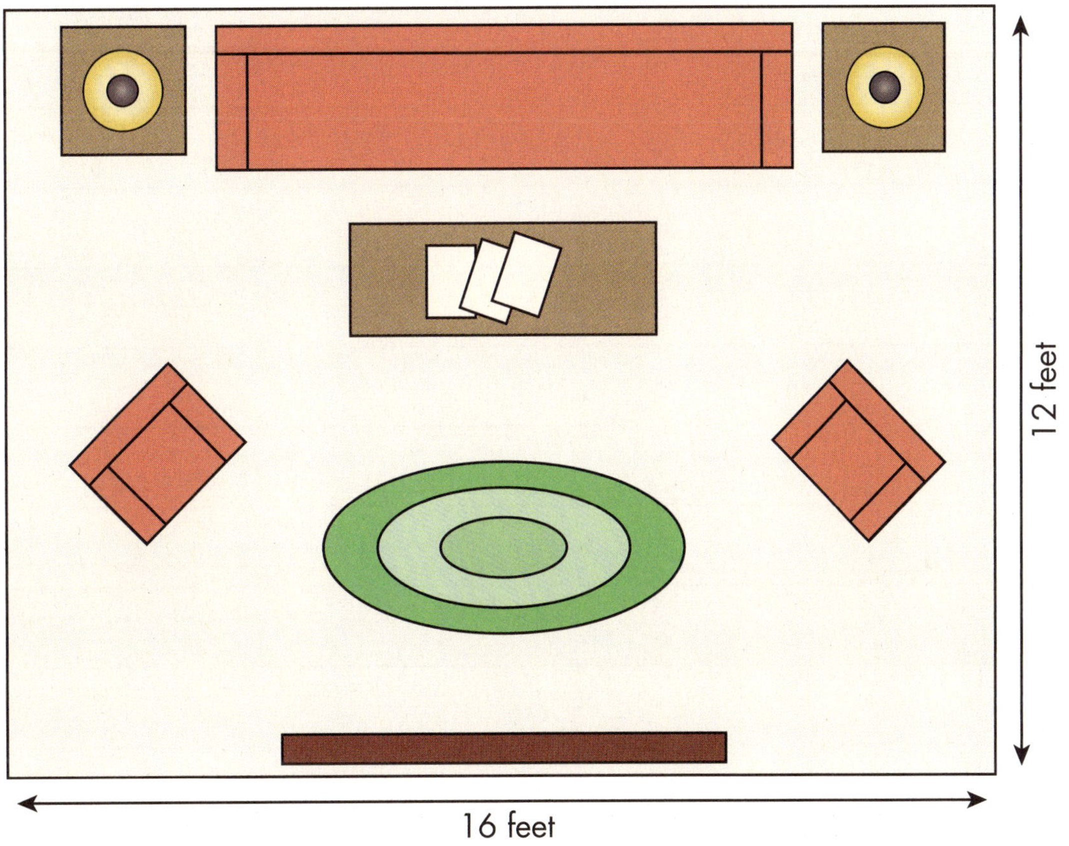

12 feet

16 feet

LESSON 22

UNIT 3 Writing

99

© The Continental Press, Inc.   DUPLICATING THIS MATERIAL IS ILLEGAL.

FOLDER B

Area

WRITING: Academic Mathematics

Check your writing. Ask yourself:

☐ Does my writing make sense?

☐ Did I write in complete sentences?

☐ Did I use correct punctuation and spelling?

☐ Did I write my best?

WRITING: Academic Science

States of Matter

Look at the diagram of the water cycle. It shows the different states of water as it moves through the water cycle.

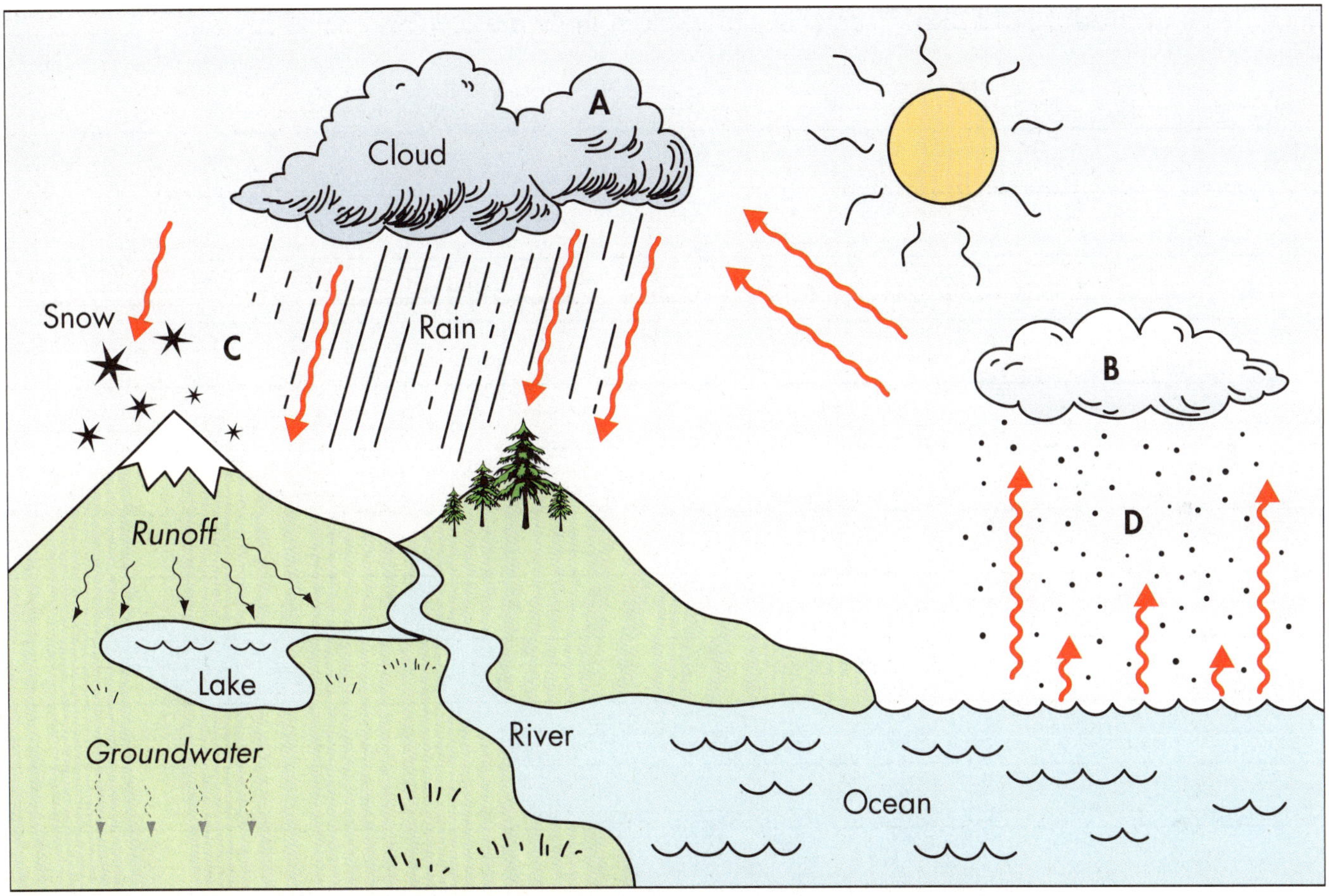

Word Box

A condense—to change from a vapor to a liquid

B evaporate—to change from liquid to a vapor

C precipitation—water that falls to the ground as rain or snow

D vapor—a gas

LESSON 23   UNIT 3 Writing   101

WRITING: Academic Science

States of Matter

Now it's time to write!

Look at the diagram. How does water move through the water cycle? Where does it go? How does water change as it moves? Write a paragraph of 5 to 7 sentences to explain the water cycle.

___

Check your writing. Ask yourself:

☐ Does my writing make sense?

☐ Did I write in complete sentences?

☐ Did I use correct punctuation and spelling?

☐ Did I write my best?

102 | **UNIT 3 Writing** | **LESSON 23**

© The Continental Press, Inc. **DUPLICATING THIS MATERIAL IS ILLEGAL.**

WRITING: Conversational Language and Academic Language Arts

Leisure Activities

Ways to Have Fun with Friends

Adults don't want kids to watch too much television or play too many computer games. So what other choices do kids have?

You and your friends can learn new games. Some games can be played inside, and some games can be played outside. There are books in the library that tell about games from other countries. You can also find games on the Internet.

You and your friends can put on a play. You can write a script, decide who will play each part, and make props and costumes. After you practice, you can invite your families to watch the play.

 **WRITING: Conversational Language and Academic Language Arts**

Leisure Activities

Now it's time to write!

Prepare to write a composition about fun activities you would do with a friend who is visiting you for the whole day. Think about what you could do inside and what you could do outside.

1 Prepare Your Ideas

Use these questions to help you gather ideas for your writing.

What kinds of activities do you and your friend like to do?

What is an activity you could do in the morning?

What activity could you do in the afternoon?

What is an activity you could do after dinner?

Turn to the next page to make a plan for writing.

WRITING: Conversational Language and Academic Language Arts

Leisure Activities

2 Plan Your Writing

Organize your ideas here. You can write notes, use a graphic organizer, or make an outline. Be sure that your plan includes

An introduction,

    The morning's activities and details,

    The afternoon's activities and details,

    The evening's activities and details,

A conclusion.

WRITING: Conversational Language and Academic Language Arts

Leisure Activities

3 Write Your Composition

Write a composition of five paragraphs telling about fun activities you and your friend will do for a whole day. Use your answers to the questions on page 104 and the ideas you wrote on page 105 to help you.

When you are finished, remember to review the checklist on page 108. The questions are important. They will help you to do your best work.

_____
_____
_____
_____
_____
_____
_____
_____
_____
_____
_____
_____
_____
_____
_____
_____

 WRITING: Conversational Language and Academic Language Arts

Leisure Activities

WRITING: Conversational Language and Academic Language Arts

Leisure Activities

_____
_____
_____
_____
_____
_____
_____
_____
_____
_____

Check your writing. Ask yourself:

☐ Did I write an introduction?

☐ Did I include three examples?

☐ Did I write a conclusion?

☐ Did I write in complete sentences?

☐ Did I use correct punctuation and spelling?

☐ Did I reread my work to make sure it made sense?

WRITING: Conversational Language

Directions

This is how to go from school to the food store. Go out the front door of the school. Turn right. Go down School Lane. Turn left onto Main Street. The food store is on the left.

WRITING: Conversational Language

Directions

Now it's time to write!

Alan is going to a birthday party after school. First, he has to go to the toy store to buy a gift. Then he will go to the party at the apartment building on Route 24. Write 5 or 6 sentences giving directions to Alan. Tell him how to go from school to the toy store. Then tell him how to go from the toy store to the apartment building.

_____
_____
_____
_____
_____
_____
_____
_____
_____

Check your writing. Ask yourself:

☐ Does my writing make sense?

☐ Did I write in complete sentences?

☐ Did I use correct punctuation and spelling?

☐ Did I write my best?

UNIT 3 Writing — LESSON 25

WRITING: Academic Mathematics

Percent

Comparing Percents

Percent is one way to tell about parts of a whole. Percent is a ratio. It tells how many out of one hundred. Using percent makes comparing parts of wholes easier.

Two soccer teams are going to have an end of the year party together. Members of each team voted for their favorite food. The pie charts show the results of voting as percents. The party planners will compare the information in the two charts. Then, they will decide what foods to have at the party.

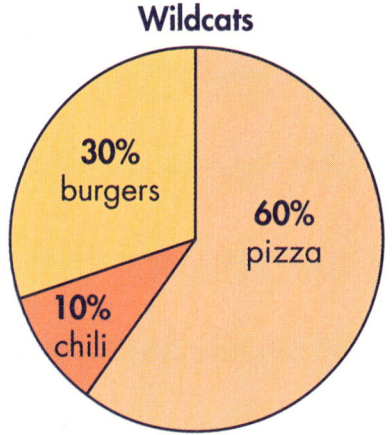
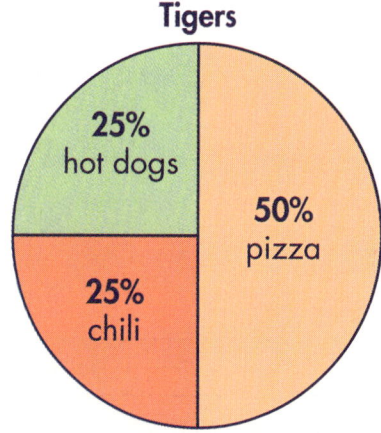

The party planners began to think about what foods to have at the party. This is how they began to write their plan:

Thirty percent of the Wildcats like burgers, but none of the Tigers like burgers. So, we will...

_____

LESSON 26   UNIT 3 Writing   111

WRITING: **Academic Mathematics**

Percent

Now it's time to write!

Imagine you are on the food committee for a picnic for 4th and 5th graders. Members of each class voted for their favorite sandwich. Compare the voting results in the charts below. You can have only three kinds of sandwiches at this event. What sandwiches would you serve? Why?

Use the pictures below and the model on page 111 to prepare your answer. Write your paragraph on the next page.

1.
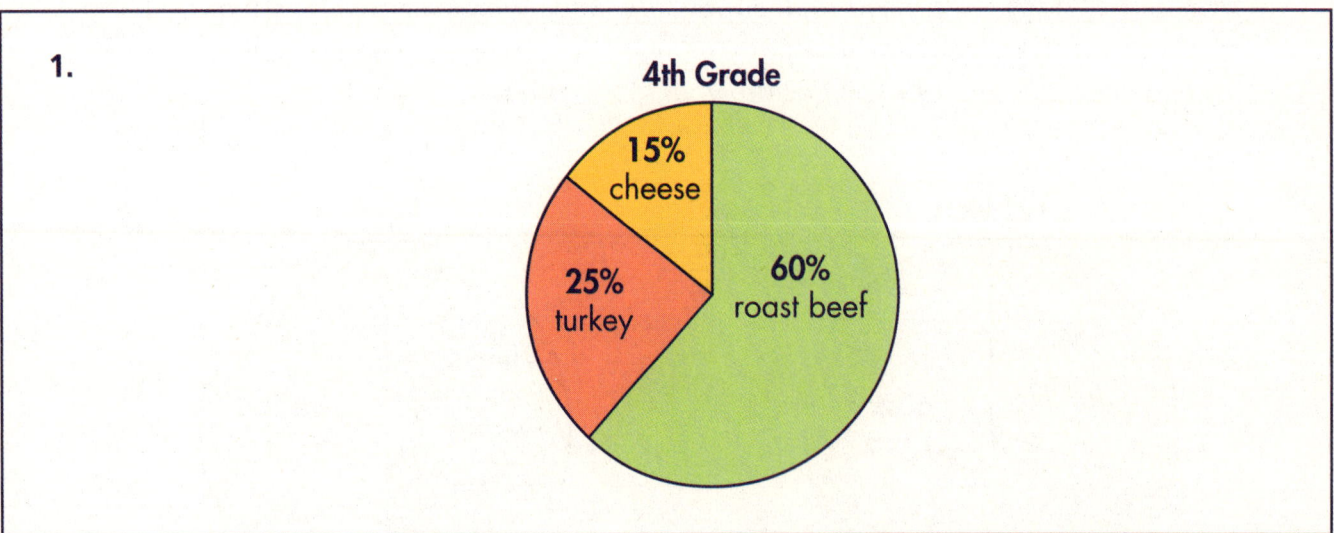

2.
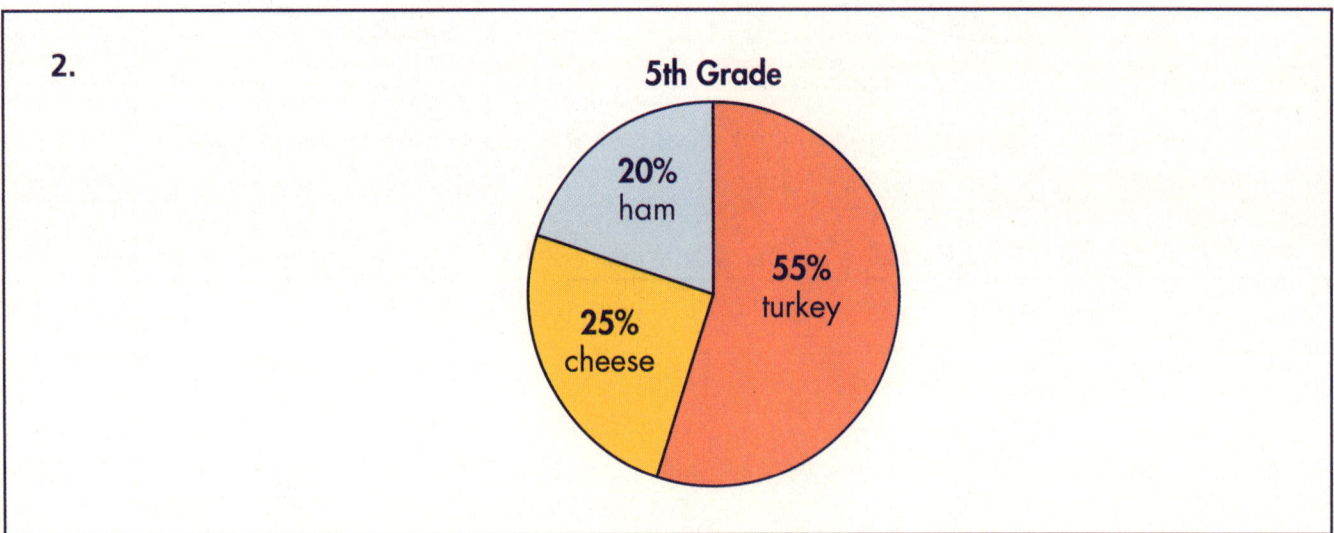

112 UNIT 3 Writing LESSON 26

WRITING: Academic Mathematics

Percent

_____
_____
_____
_____
_____
_____
_____
_____
_____
_____
_____
_____
_____
_____

Check your writing. Ask yourself:

- ☐ Did I compare the voting results to make my choices?
- ☐ Does my writing make sense?
- ☐ Did I write in complete sentences?
- ☐ Did I use correct punctuation and spelling?
- ☐ Did I write my best?

WRITING: Academic Science

Body Systems

The Human Respiratory System

Your body needs oxygen. Your respiratory system brings oxygen into your body from the air. The respiratory system puts the oxygen into your blood. The heart pumps the blood and oxygen throughout your body. The blood brings back carbon dioxide, and the respiratory system gets rid of it.

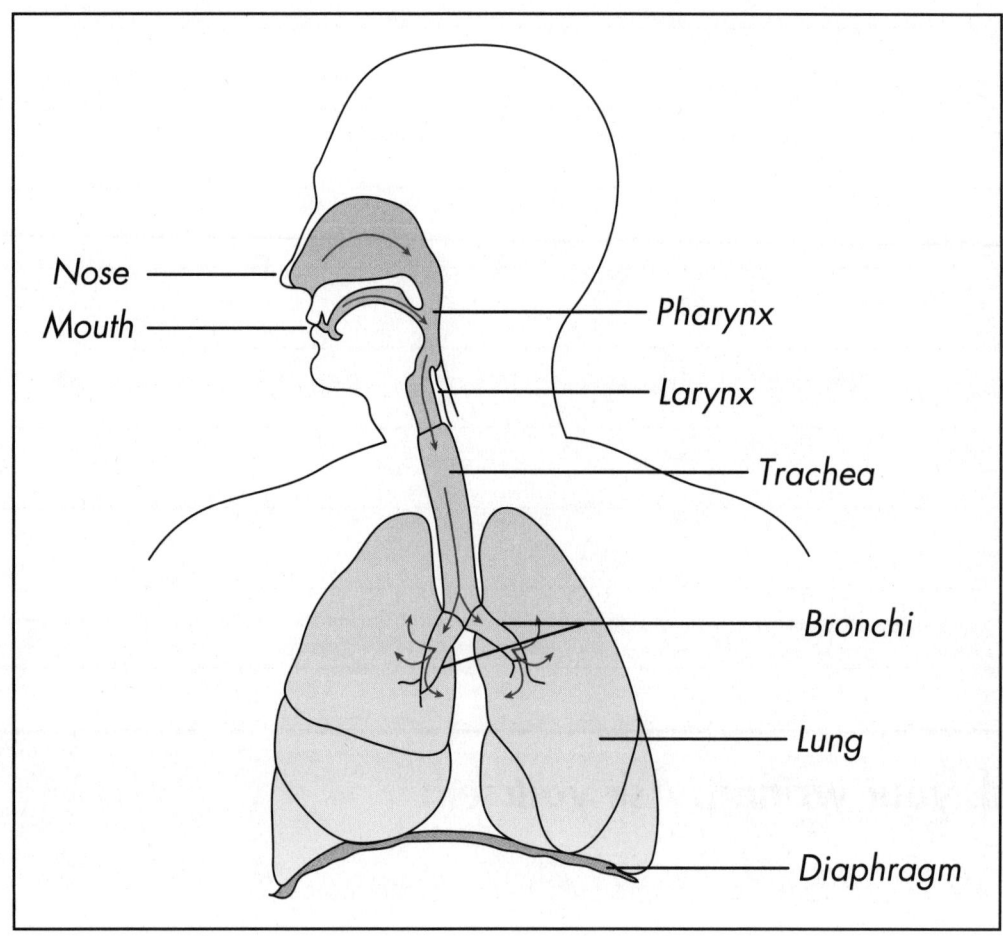

WRITING: Academic Science

Body Systems

Now it's time to write!

Think about what you know about the respiratory system. Look at the diagram. Write a paragraph of 5 to 7 sentences to tell how the respiratory system works.

___
___
___
___
___
___
___
___
___
___

Check your writing. Ask yourself:

☐ Did I explain how the respiratory system works?

☐ Does my writing make sense?

☐ Did I write in complete sentences?

☐ Did I use correct punctuation and spelling?

☐ Did I write my best?

WRITING: Academic Language Arts and Social Studies

Basic Economics

Read the article. Pay attention to the examples listed. Think about the kinds of goods and services people in your community provide.

Goods and Services

Goods

Goods are things we need or want. Some people make goods. For example, farmers grow crops and raise animals for food. Fishermen catch fish, clams, crabs, and shrimp. Cooks and bakers take some of the crops and animals to prepare foods for people to buy.

Workers in huge factories make some of the goods we need. Workers make the clothing we wear, the toys we play with, the cars we drive, the televisions we watch, and many other kinds of goods.

We pay for the goods we buy. The people who make the goods use the money we pay them to buy goods and services they need.

Services

Services are actions people do for us. The teacher who teaches you provides a service. The dentist who cleans your teeth provides a service. The president who leads our country provides a service.

We pay people to provide services for us. The people who provide the services use the money to buy the goods and services they need.

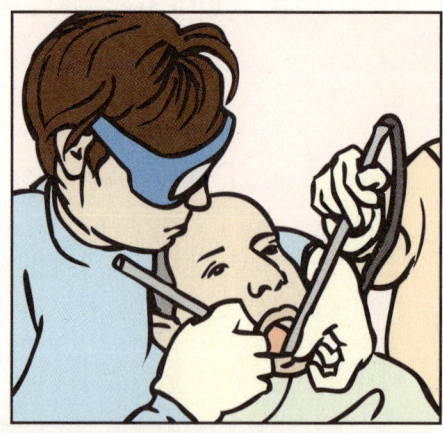

116   UNIT 3 Writing   LESSON 28

© The Continental Press, Inc.   **DUPLICATING THIS MATERIAL IS ILLEGAL.**

WRITING: Academic Language Arts and Social Studies

Basic Economics

Now it's time to write!

Think about the facts you read in "Goods and Services." Now, imagine you are a newspaper reporter. You have been assigned to write an article about jobs in your community that provide goods and services.

1 Prepare Your Ideas

Use these questions to help you gather ideas for your writing.

What jobs will I write about?

What goods do they produce?

What services do they provide?

Who uses these goods and services?

Why are these goods and services important?

Turn to the next page to make a plan for writing.

WRITING: Academic Language Arts and Social Studies

Basic Economics

2 Plan Your Writing

Organize your ideas here. You can write notes, use a graphic organizer, or make an outline. Be sure that your plan includes

An introduction that tells what goods and services are,

Two examples of jobs in your community that produce goods,

Details that describe these goods,

Two examples of jobs in your community that provide services,

Details that describe these services,

A conclusion that gives reasons why these goods and services are important for your community.

WRITING: Academic Language Arts and Social Studies

Basic Economics

3 Write Your Essay

Write a four-paragraph essay about jobs in your community that provide goods and services. Use your answers to the questions on page 117 and the ideas you wrote on page 118 to help you.

When you are finished, remember to review the checklist on page 120. The questions are important. They will help you to do your best work.

WRITING: Academic Language Arts and Social Studies

Basic Economics

_____
_____
_____
_____
_____
_____
_____
_____
_____
_____

Check your writing. Ask yourself:

☐ Did I write an essay?

☐ Did I organize my ideas in four paragraphs?

☐ Did I tell about jobs in my community?

☐ Did I include details about the goods and services those jobs provide?

☐ Did I write in complete sentences?

☐ Did I use correct punctuation and spelling?

☐ Did I reread my work to make sure it made sense?

UNIT 4 SPEAKING

Each lesson in this unit focuses on a specific content topic or topics:

1. Conversational language
2. The language of Academic Language Arts
3. The language of Academic Mathematics
4. The language of Academic Science
5. The language of Academic Social Studies

In this unit, you will:

- look at a picture or pictures
- find information and vocabulary in the picture
- listen to and understand a question asked by your teacher
- answer a series of questions about the pictures
- use the picture clues to help answer the questions

Speak clearly and try to do the best you can!

Model Lesson

ACADEMIC SCIENCE: Animals in Our Neighborhood

UNIT 4 Speaking

SPEAKING: Conversational Language

Personal Experiences

Part 1

Sometimes, families like to do things outdoors. A parent and a child might go to a pond. They might see water birds on the pond. This little girl and her father watch water birds called geese. They have fun at the pond.

SPEAKING: Conversational Language

Personal Experiences

Part 2

People like to take their family pets outdoors. People take their pets outdoors to give them exercise. They take their pets outdoors to play. This girl is playing with her dog. She is using a toy called a Frisbee.

SPEAKING: Conversational Language

Personal Experiences

Part 3

![pool photo]

Some families play in water. They go to pools, rivers, or the ocean. There are a lot of activities to do in the water. People can swim, dive, or play games. It is important to be safe in the water.

SPEAKING: Academic Language Arts and Social Studies

Historical Figures

Part 1

Thomas Jefferson lived from 1743 to 1826. One of the most important things he did was help to write the Declaration of Independence. At that time, Great Britain owned the place we now call the United States. The Declaration of Independence said that the people here wanted to be free. It said the people could pick their own leaders and make their own laws. The people of the United States declared that they would not obey the laws of Great Britain.

126 UNIT 4 Speaking LESSON 30

© The Continental Press, Inc. DUPLICATING THIS MATERIAL IS ILLEGAL.

SPEAKING: Academic Language Arts and Social Studies

Historical Figures

Part 2

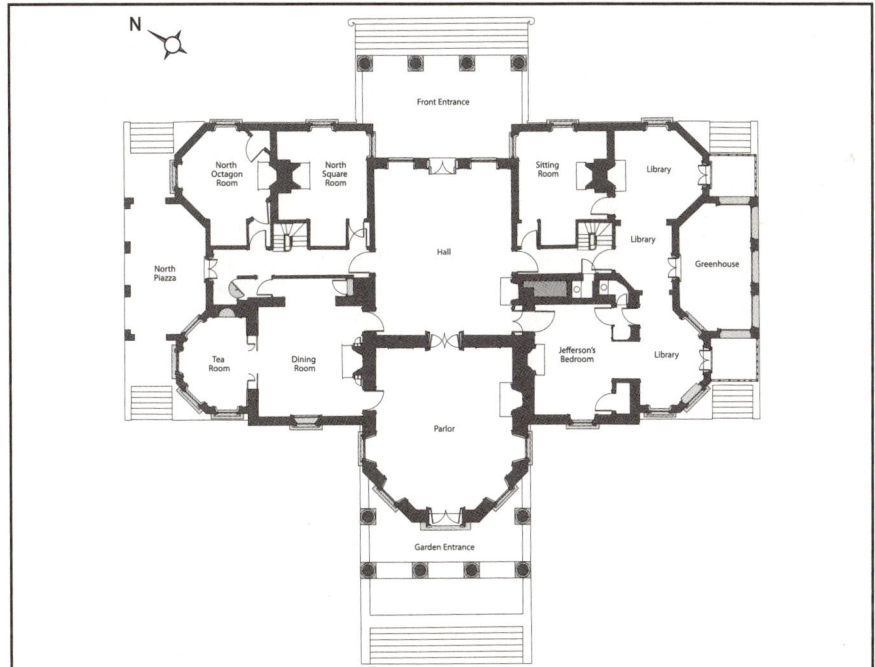

Thomas Jefferson loved to read. He had thousands of books at his home called Monticello. There was a huge library in Monticello. By 1814, Jefferson owned more books than any other American. He read books to learn about the world.

SPEAKING: Academic Language Arts and Social Studies

Historical Figures

Part 3

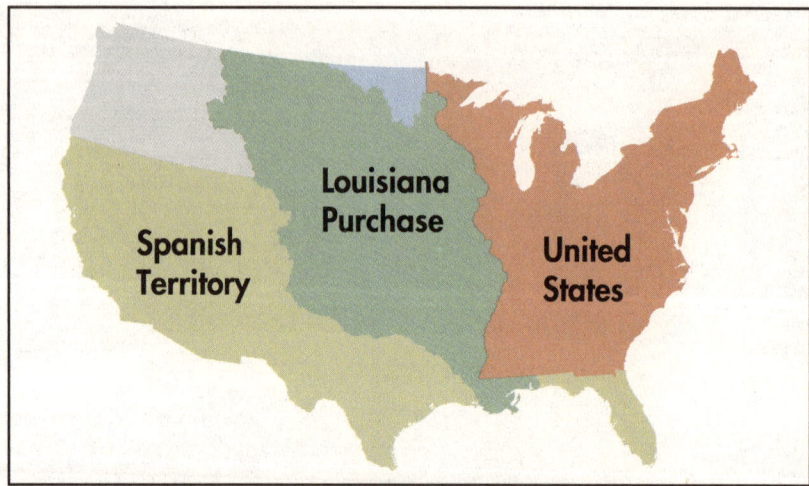

Thomas Jefferson was the third president of the United States. He was the president from 1801 until 1809. One important thing he did as president was buy land known as the Louisiana Purchase. This new land made the United States much bigger. Then Jefferson asked two men to explore the land. They were Meriwether Lewis and William Clark. They saw rivers, land, and people of the area. An American Indian named Sacagawea helped them.

SPEAKING: Academic Language Arts and Social Studies

Historical Figures

Part 4

Thomas Jefferson also invented things. An inventor makes new tools to solve problems or make work easier. Thomas Jefferson thought farming was very important. He grew flowers, vegetables, and fruits at Monticello. In his time, people used plows pulled by horses to dig up the soil to plant. Jefferson made a better plow. It dug the soil more easily, and the horses did not have to work as hard. He also invented a bookstand. It could hold five books at once. It could also spin around. Then it could be folded up into a box.

SPEAKING: Academic Language Arts and Social Studies

Historical Figures

Part 5

The Jefferson Memorial honors Thomas Jefferson as a great American. The memorial is in Washington, D. C. The building is made in a circular shape that Jefferson liked for buildings. It has a statue of Jefferson inside. The statue is 19 feet high. That is taller than three humans. The building and statue were finished in 1943. Many people visit the Jefferson Memorial each year.

SPEAKING: Academic Mathematics and Science

Food and Nutrition

Part 1

Nutrient	Food Examples
carbohydrates	grains, fruits, potatoes, squash
protein	meat, fish, yogurt, nuts
fats	oils, meats, cheese, nuts, fish

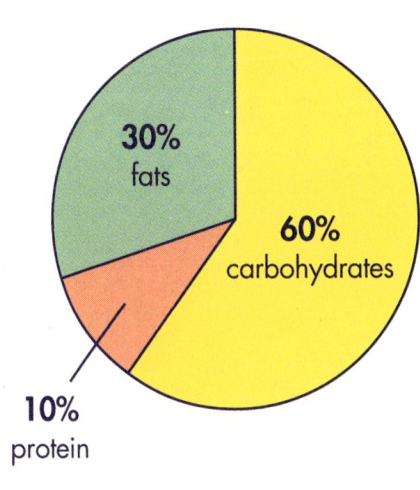

There are three things we need in our diet to stay healthy. We need carbohydrates, protein, and fats. These are called nutrients. They help us grow. They help us to stay well and to get better if we are sick.

SPEAKING: **Academic Mathematics and Science**

Food and Nutrition

Part 2

A food label shows what nutrients are in the food. It tells the amount of nutrients, such as 1 gram of fat. A gram is a unit of measure. Grams tell how much something weighs. A label also tells a percent. For example, a label may say, "Total carbohydrates 2%." That means one serving of the food has two percent of the carbohydrates we need for a whole day.

SPEAKING: Academic Mathematics and Science

Food and Nutrition

Part 3

Fast Food Breakfast Sandwich

Total Fat	33 grams	50%
Total Carbohydrates	43 grams	14%
Protein	20 grams	40%

Oatmeal

Total Fat	2 grams	4%
Total Carbohydrates	26 grams	9%
Protein	4 grams	8%

We can compare the percents on two food labels to decide which food is best for us. We should choose foods that give us the nutrients we need to stay healthy and grow strong. Our diets should be balanced to give us each nutrient in every meal. We should not get too much of one nutrient, for example fat, at one meal.

SPEAKING: Academic Mathematics and Science

Food and Nutrition

Part 4

Spaghetti (one serving)

Total Fat	$1\frac{1}{2}$ grams	2%
Total Carbohydrates	42 grams	14%
Protein	7 grams	14%

Meat Sauce (one serving)

Total Fat	5 grams	8%
Total Carbohydrates	19 grams	6%
Protein	2 grams	4%

Cheese (one serving)

Total Fat	$1\frac{1}{2}$ grams	2%
Total Carbohydrates	less than 1 gram	0%
Protein	2 grams	14%

We can use several ingredients to make a meal. Each ingredient has nutrients. We can figure out how many nutrients the meal has altogether. Labels can help a cook figure out what nutrients are in a spaghetti dinner.

SPEAKING: Academic Mathematics and Science

Food and Nutrition

Part 5

Sodium is another word for salt. Sodium is important to our health. It helps our muscles and nerves work properly. However, some people get too much sodium in their diets. We should not have more than 2,400 milligrams of sodium a day. A milligram is a measure that tells how much. For example, 2,400 milligrams of salt is about 1.6 teaspoons. We can use nutrition labels to be sure we do not get too much sodium.

LESSON 31   UNIT 4 Speaking   135

SPEAKING: Conversational Language

Health and Safety

Part 1

One way to stay healthy is to exercise. We need to move our bodies. Exercise keeps our bodies strong. There are many kinds of exercise. We can run, ride bikes, play sports, or jump rope. All of these activities help us stay healthy.

SPEAKING: Conversational Language

Health and Safety

Part 2

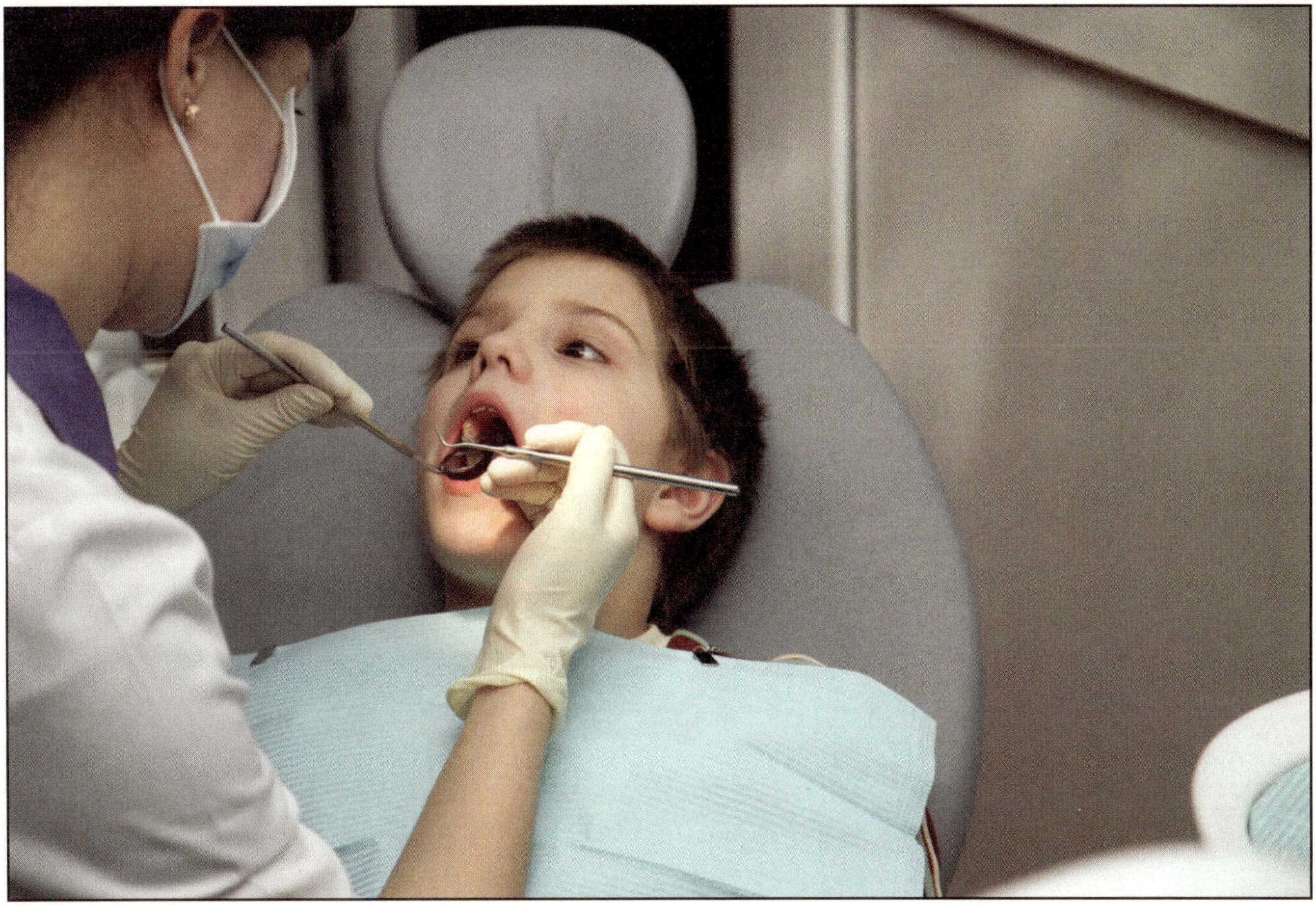

Doctors help us take care of our bodies. Doctors tell us how to eat and exercise to stay well. Doctors also help us when we are sick or hurt. They help us fix problems with our bodies. There are many kinds of doctors. There are doctors that help with different parts of our bodies, such as our eyes, our teeth, and our lungs.

SPEAKING: Conversational Language

Health and Safety

Part 3

Good food is very important. It helps our bodies grow. Good food also helps us fight off sickness. Families can make healthful meals at home. They can use nutritional foods such as fruits and vegetables. Families should be sure to eat different kinds of foods instead of eating the same things over and over. Sometimes, families work together to make healthy meals.

SPEAKING: Academic Language Arts and Social Studies

Communities and Regions

Part 1

The Navajo are American Indians. The desert where many Navajo people live has many landforms. In the picture, you see can see a canyon. A canyon is a narrow place between steep walls of stone.

◀ LESSON 33   **UNIT 4 Speaking**   139

 SPEAKING: **Academic Language Arts and Social Studies**

Communities and Regions

Part 2

Navajo people have raised sheep for hundreds of years. The women use wool from the sheep to weave rugs. The sheep eat grass near the river. The people also have a garden where they raise corn, squash, and other vegetables.

 SPEAKING: Academic Language Arts and Social Studies

Communities and Regions

Part 3

People all over the world make music. The Navajo love music, too. They hold different kinds of gatherings to make music. One special gathering is for couples to sing and dance. They have contests, and the best singers and dancers win prizes. Everyone gets dressed up to go to a "Song and Dance."

SPEAKING: **Academic Language Arts and Social Studies**

Communities and Regions

Part 4

Some Navajo rugs tell stories. They may show scenes of everyday life. They may show what it is like to live on the reservation.

 SPEAKING: Academic Language Arts and Social Studies

Communities and Regions

Part 5

Today, many Navajo people live on the reservation. Others live in big cities such as Phoenix. The reservation offers Navajo people their land, their traditions, and their community. Cities offer more jobs and a more modern way of living.

SPEAKING: Academic Mathematics and Science

Weather Patterns

Part 1

Weather Statistics for Honolulu, Hawaii

	January	February	March
Temperature	73 degrees	75 degrees	74 degrees
Precipitation	$3\frac{1}{2}$ inches	$2\frac{1}{2}$ inches	3 inches

People keep records about the weather. Scientists who study weather use a special language. The language is called descriptive statistics. Descriptive statistics help us understand and talk about weather data. Data is information shown usually in numbers. Descriptive statistics help us compare weather at different times to notice patterns. Two kinds of weather data are temperature and precipitation. Temperature is how hot or cold the air is. There are two measures of temperature. They are Fahrenheit and Celsius. The temperatures in this lesson are Fahrenheit. Precipitation is rain, snow, sleet, or hail.

 SPEAKING: Academic Mathematics and Science

Weather Patterns

Part 2

Monday

	Temperature	Wind speed	Wind chill
6 A.M.	25°F	10 miles per hour	Feels like 15°F
9 A.M.	35°F	30 miles per hour	Feels like 22°F
Noon	40°F	15 miles per hour	Feels like 32°F
3 P.M.	40°F	10 miles per hour	Feels like 34°F
6 P.M.	32°F	15 miles per hour	Feels like 15°F

We can also talk about the mode to describe weather statistics. The mode is the number that we see most often in a set of data.

SPEAKING: Academic Mathematics and Science

Weather Patterns

Part 3

	Mon.	Tues.	Wed.	Thurs.	Fri.
High Temperature	54°F	63°F	74°F	57°F	55°F
Low temperature	35°F	34°F	43°F	42°F	44°F
Wind (miles per hour)	10	4	5	8	10
Humidity	37%	29%	70%	83%	23%
Precipitation (inches)	0	0	$\frac{1}{2}$	$\frac{3}{4}$	0

Another way to talk about weather data is to identify the median. A median is the middle number or amount. There are two steps to figure out median. First, you arrange the numbers from highest to lowest or lowest to highest. Then you see which number falls in the middle.

SPEAKING: Academic Mathematics and Science

Weather Patterns

Part 4

Weather Data for Cities in Southeast Texas

	Austin	Corpus Christi	Houston
High temperature	80°F	81°F	79°F
Low temperature	59°F	62°F	60°F
Precipitation (inches)	32	30	51
Clear days	116	136	91

The mean is another way to describe data. Another word for mean is average. We figure the mean by adding figures and dividing by the number of figures we added. When scientists calculate mean temperatures and mean precipitation, it helps them see what the weather was like over time. It helps them notice patterns over months and years.

SPEAKING: Academic Mathematics and Science

Weather Patterns

Part 5

	2000	2002	2004	2006	2008
Mean High Temperate	63°F	64°F	68°F	59°F	64°F
Mean Low Temperature	41°F	40°F	42°F	41°F	42°F
Mean Precipitation (inches)	12	11	10	6	8

Scientists look at weather statistics over the years to see patterns. Patterns help scientists predict weather. They help us know if the climate of a place is changing. Climate is the average weather in a place over time.

NOTES

NOTES